H4439

LANGUAGE AND
CHRISTIAN BELIEF

LANGUAGE AND CHRISTIAN BELIEF

BY

JOHN WILSON

LONDON

MACMILLAN & CO LTD

NEW YORK · ST MARTIN'S PRESS

1958

MACMILLAN AND COMPANY LIMITED
London Bombay Calcutta Madras Melbourne

THE MACMILLAN COMPANY OF CANADA LIMITED
Toronto

ST MARTIN'S PRESS INC
New York

PRINTED IN GREAT BRITAIN

CONTENTS

ACKNOWLEDGEMENTS

I SHOULD like to make my acknowledgements, with sincere gratitude, to those who have helped in various ways to make this book possible: to Mr. S. Hampshire, Professor R. B. Braithwaite, Professor A. Flew, the Revd. P. E. Wilson, Dr. F. J. Shirley, and Mr. R. Davy: and also to the Revd. L. A. Garrard, for permission to reprint material published in the *Hibbert Journal*.

J. B. W.

INTRODUCTION

The phrase 'philosophy of religion' is still used to refer to an important field of study. But today the area of that field is not marked out with any precision. That it has changed, and is still changing, is evident from a comparison of standard works on the subject written more than thirty years ago with those written today; yet it is still far from clear what the philosopher of religion is supposed to be doing. This lack of clarity at a high intellectual level is only one symptom of a general, though I hope only temporary, failure on the part of religious believers to meet an important challenge. Part of my purpose is to make the nature of this challenge clear.

What has changed in the last few decades is not religion, but philosophy. Predominantly in England and Amerca but also in other countries, the word 'philosophy' has taken on an entirely new meaning. It no longer implies wisdom, or an advanced insight into reality, or an enlarged knowledge of the natural and supernatural worlds around us. The typical philosopher in a British or American university does not claim the powers of a sage. To be sure, he is still concerned with truth; but he is not concerned in the same way as his predecessors. It is commonly said that he is concerned only with language: and the phrase 'linguistic philosophy', like 'logical positivist', is widely used by laymen. But this view misses most of the point. Modern philosophers are concerned, not with the facts of the world around us—this is the scientist's business — but with our understanding and communication of facts. They are concerned to ensure that this understanding and communication is not vitiated by a lack of logic or confusion of thought. This is why they spend so much time on the study of language; for truths are expressed in language. It is not things or persons that we call 'true', but statements[1] and consequently philosophers examine statements in order to discover what type of statements they are, and what sort of truth they are supposed to express. They are also interested, not so much in whether or not there is any actual evidence for these statements, but in what would count as evidence. Hence their perpetual concern with verification and meaning.

Whether or not we choose to use the word 'philosophy' for this activity alone, it is evident that the activity is a necessary one; and whether or not only those who engage in it are to be called 'philosophers', we cannot afford to disregard their work and conclusions. Religious statements and religious language are not exempted from rational criticism; and where such criticism strikes at the root of religious belief as a whole, as I shall try to show that it does, it is intellectual suicide not to take it seriously. Many people still think, mistakenly, that modern philosophy represents merely a passing phase, and that Christianity can afford to let its arrows glance off the helmets of the faithful. There

[1] We can, of course, speak of billiard-tables 'running true', of 'a good man and true', etc.: but the general point remains. Failure to understand that truth is predicated primarily of beliefs and statements has resulted in many misconceived attempts in metaphysics: many of them, unfortunately, undertaken by Christian writers. See my *Language and the Pursuit of Truth*, Chapter III (C.U.P., 1956).

are others who grant intellectual acceptance to its conclusions, without seriously applying them to their own beliefs: thus, perhaps, meriting the charge of 'double-think' levelled at them by some writers. Others again are seriously worried by the conclusions, but seem either unwilling or unable to show how they can be made to square with religious doctrine.

Unfortunately the professional philosophers afford us little help here. Very few of them are concerned to defend or interpret the Christian faith in the light of their professional knowledge, though plenty of them are concerned to query it or denounce it. Their questions, however, are penetrating and demanding, and represent a challenge which seems more fundamental and more difficult to meet than any previous challenge. Christianity has (perhaps rather belatedly) met the Darwinian or scientific challenge, and survived. It has met and survived countless others. But it has not done so by magic: it has done so by hard thinking on the part of Christians. To put the radical nature of this new challenge briefly, it is not that the actual truth of or evidence for individual statements in religious belief is being questioned, as for instance was the case with the Creation story in Genesis: it is rather that the whole meaning and verification of religious statements comes under fire. In brief, philosophers say something like: 'What does so-and-so mean exactly? What sort of statement is it? What standards of evidence are relevant to assessing its truth, and what would count as proof or disproof? In particular, what would count as decisive evidence against it?' Taken in conjunction with certain modern philosophical conclusions, the answers given to these questions by Christian writers have not been very satisfactory. Yet plainly they are questions to which Christians should have satisfactory answers: for they are not technical questions asked by logical pedants, but straightforward questions which could be asked (and I believe are being asked in a rather more indirect way) by quite ordinary people.

The days when some philosophers used to declare all religious and metaphysical statements to be 'meaningless' are now long past. Most of the efforts of philosophers are now devoted to trying to discover what sort of meaning or use they have; but unfortunately none of these efforts is accepted by Christians as giving a satisfactory account of their faith. Christian writers, on the other hand, very properly spend a great deal of time in rebutting philosophical attacks on parts of the faith, but these rebuttals at best merely preserve ground long held, and do little to bring the two combatants together. Christians have yet to provide answers to these philosophical questions: they may repel individual bullets, but they do not seem able to bring about a cease-fire.

It is not to be expected, of course, that Christianity should have an immediate answer up its sleeve for any and every question that may be fired at it. But it is reasonable to hope that the faith should be shown not just to evade, but to stand up to philosophical attack, and it is unfortunately true that in many philosophical circles the impression conveyed by Christian apologists—rightly or wrongly — is one of evasion. They seem to want to preserve the faith at all costs, even at the price of irrationality. If that were true, of course, the philosopher would be entitled to wash his hands of the whole business; for he deals only in the rationality or justifiability of beliefs, not in their psychological effects: in what is true, not in what is morally or psychologically uplifting or comforting. But I think the impression is largely false.

I hope as well as believe that the impression is largely false, because the philosophical challenge to Christianity is considerably more serious than my rather brief and necessarily superficial survey would suggest. There are two points which I believe that every Christian should fully appreciate. One of them is logical, and the other sociological: both are essential.

1. There is a prevalent impression that Christianity *need* not engage the philosophers: that the onus is on the philosophers to disprove the doctrines of the Christian faith if they can, but that since they have not succeeded as yet, it is not part of a Christian's duty to take them seriously. This might have been true in the past, when philosophy was concerned with putting forward various moral and metaphysical beliefs of its own: such beliefs might represent merely alternatives to the Christian faith, not radical challenges to it. But today the position is entirely altered. For the modern philosophical challenge is not that Christian beliefs are untrue — or at least not directly this — but rather that they have no certain meaning.

Imagine two situations: (i) a man makes a statement: his hearer understands him, but disagrees. The first man can produce all the evidence, evidence which is admitted by both to be relevant: after this, he can reasonably say: 'Well, there's my evidence: take it or leave it.' (ii) A man makes a statement: his hearer does not understand him at all. His hearer says: 'Whatever in the world do you mean?

I don't understand a word you say.' If the man tries to bring forward evidence, his hearer says: 'It's no good, I can't possibly tell whether this is genuine evidence or not unless I can understand what you mean first. At present what you say is just so many words to me: I don't at all see what these words are supposed to *do*: what they are supposed to refer to, or how the statements they contain could ever, in principle, be shown to be true.' Christianity is in the second position, and not in the first. And it is reasonable to say that, whereas in position (i) the onus is on the hearer to consider the evidence, think about it, and so on, in position (ii) the onus is on the speaker to say what he means, so that his beliefs may be publicly assessed, and to provide some method of assessment. Otherwise the hearer would be entitled to dismiss them, not necessarily as false, but as undiscussible. And this is precisely what some people are beginning to do with Christian beliefs today. They are perishing by default.

2. The sociological point has been made very frequently in various forms, but is still not fully appreciated. Some Christians still believe that the intellectual basis of Christianity does not matter except to intellectuals: that it is not sociologically important, only logically so. I think that many authorities would deny this; and therefore it is worth enlarging upon the point.

This belief, also, may have been true in the past. It may be true, as thinkers from Bacon onwards have suggested, that the waxing and waning of religious faith is due, not to the rooting of such faith in reason, but to psychological factors, of which individual and social security is perhaps the most important. When men feel frightened, insecure, or discontented, they turn to religion. They are prepared to accept metaphysical beliefs, obey and look up to religious authorities, and adhere to religious ritual. They may also adopt a religious morality. But when things look brighter, and people are contented and secure, they lose something of the awe and humility which lie at the root of most religions. They become independent, self-satisfied, confident and perhaps proud: it is then that they say things like: 'We no longer need religion.' They may adopt some kind of substitute: the progress of the physical sciences and the security they bring with them, or advanced psychological and psychiatric knowledge. All this may be partly inevitable: a natural fluctuation due to historic forces which we cannot entirely control.

Even if this deterministic picture were entirely lifelike, however, the importance of rational belief is still demonstrated. For it means that we can no longer browbeat, bludgeon, terrify or otherwise irrationally induce belief: we can no longer rely upon awe and reverence, material insecurity and uncertainty, to do an evangelical job for us. The reason for this is that today, particularly in the western world and to an increasing extent wherever western technology is spreading, the rise of science and education has engendered a greater feeling of material and mental security — even though we may suspect that this security is partially unreal, and has no abiding roots. The point is that people now no longer *feel* that they need religion to the same extent, even where they pay lip-service to it. This feeling may be mistaken. But it exists. And the net result of all this is that men today, particularly in countries where the standard of education is high, insist upon a more rational approach than they used to demand. No doubt the basic insecurity which must exist without religion has only gone underground: I think this is particularly true of our attitude to death, to take but one example. But it remains true that if Christians are to sustain and enlarge the boundaries of Christ's empire, they will not achieve very much by moral pressure or irrational methods alone. Preaching is important, but preaching to people who are not there is hardly effective evangelism. Teaching is more likely to succeed: though of course the two are not mutually exclusive.

People today (one must generalise for the sake of brevity) will, in fact, question and criticise Christian belief by any available means. This is a fact that must be faced. If we say, like the man in our example, 'take it or leave it,' we cannot be sure that they will not leave it. Moreover, as we have seen, a 'take it or leave it' attitude is inappropriate to the type of questioning involved. Failure to grasp the general sociological point which we are now making usually comprises also failure to grasp the particular point; that the philosophical challenge is not confined to a few intellectuals, but is already widespread throughout the western world. For instance, I happen to teach divinity to the Sixth Forms of a public school: and it is quite plain that the types of questions which the boys ask cannot be answered satisfactorily by anyone who is not philosophically able to do so, since they are (although this may not always be evident to the boys themselves) precisely those types of questions which modern philosophers ask. I am not now suggesting, what would be untrue as well as immodest, that only a person with modern philosophical training can bring people to Christ. But I am suggesting that what genuinely stands between many people — at school and elsewhere — and Christ is a general failure to answer these philosophical or quasi-philosophical questions; and that therefore the Church as a whole must provide answers or lose many of her flock. As modern philosophy continues to spread, the questions will become more frequent still: and as the boys grow older and wiser — particularly if they go to a university, where these questions are repeated in a clearer form — the questions will become more insistent still. It is not too much to say, though it may sound pessimistic and unlikely, that this represents a sequence whose end term may be the general extinction of Christian belief, at least amongst educated people.

The task of understanding and interpreting Christian doctrine in the light of modern philosophy has only just been begun. It is an enormous task, and will take many more and many wiser minds than myself to complete successfully: indeed, it is doubtful whether it can in principle ever be completed. But so long as Christianity does not stand still, it can survive and flourish. It is essential, however, that all Christians should face the philosophical facts fairly and squarely, and that they should adopt something of the unbiased and rationalistic temperament of the best type of agnostic: for only discussion and argument conducted in this spirit will serve the Christian evangelistic purpose. I hope that what follows will go some way towards showing that Christian apologetics can stand on their own feet, can meet the philosopher with his own weapons, and need not cloak any weaknesses by evasion, ambiguity, or failure to meet the philosophical points, be they never so sharp.

In writing this book I have set myself three tasks, and what I propose to do is this: in the first two chapters I shall examine the philosophical foundations of religious belief in general, with reference to the modern philosophical challenge. Here we shall be chiefly concerned with the meaning and verification of religious statements, and with religious experience. In the next three, I shall try to show how some of our most common opinions, and reasons for belief or disbelief in religion, fit into the framework of modern philosophy. In this section I shall be concerned with the problems presented by belief relying on authority, by the concept of 'knowing God', and by science. Finally, in the remaining chapters, I shall discuss certain specific and recurrent problems of Christian belief, in order to show what light can be shed on them by philosophy.

In this way I hope to show (i) that religious belief as a whole can be philosophically respectable; (ii) that nevertheless, if it is to be so, we must radically alter many of our most common ideas about religion; and (iii) that even when the general problems have been solved, philosophy is by no means valueless to the Christian believer, in dealing with the specific problems of his faith. Whether or not the reader regards particular arguments as convincing, however, I shall have succeeded at least in part if I persuade him that the impact of modern philosophy upon religion is something which concerns alike those of all creeds, or of no creed at all; and that some understanding of this philosophy is an essential tool for the hands of those who wish to build, and of those who wish to demolish.

1

Verification and Religious Language

Let us begin by taking a superficial glance at the language of religion. In religious works of literature, creeds, ritual, and so on we come across different types of sentences which have (or appear to have) different uses. On this superficial level, we can list these without difficulty:

1. Sentences expressing commands, injunctions, exhortations, wishes, etc., such as 'Thou shalt love the Lord thy God', 'Let us love one another', and so on.

2. Sentences expressing moral views, such as 'Brethren, these things ought not so to be', 'It is not good for man to be alone', etc.

3. Sentences expressing factual truths, often historical, such as 'Christ was born in Bethlehem', 'Mary was a virgin', etc.

4. Sentences giving information about the meanings of words, expressing analytic truths. A statement like 'A sacrament is an outward and visible sign of an inward and spiritual grace' is analytic, and should be taken as informing the hearer about the meaning of 'sacrament'.

5. Sentences which appear to be informative, but informative about the supernatural or metaphysical rather

than the natural or physical world. For instance, 'God exists', 'Christ is the Son of God', and so on.

So far the philosopher has not yet got to work. But when he does, it is likely that he will be tempted to make two changes in our scheme above. The first does not concern us here: it involves merging what I have called 'moral views' with 'commands, injunctions, etc.', at least to some extent. The second is to attempt to distribute sentences in (5), metaphysical sentences, among the other classes, in such a way that the possibility of supernaturally informative sentences is excluded. He could say, for instance, that some of these sentences are really analytic, and others really commands: this is one of the commonest ways in which this particular move is made.

Let us look, for example, at one of the ablest attempts to make this kind of move which have recently appeared. It has been made by Professor Braithwaite. He regards religious belief as primarily the intention or resolution to adopt a certain way of life, this intention being supported by what he calls 'stories': that is, what appear to be empirical statments of fact, statements about the world, which are however not verifiable in the way that ordinary empirical statements are verifiable. (Presumably the only sense in which they could be said to be verifiable at all is the sense in which we say that a statement in a story or work of fiction is verifiable, i.e. within the context of the work as a whole.) These statements are believed because the religious believer finds them psychologically helpful, inasmuch as they bolster up his intention to adopt the way of life which he has chosen. But they are not central to religious belief; and we should verify whether a man is to be regarded as adhering to or following a certain religion, not by seeing how many 'stories' or how much of any 'story' he accepts as true, but by seeing how far he genuinely tries to carry out his intention to adopt a religious way of life. This intention, according to Braithwaite, has a great deal in common with what is expressed in ethical statements. Religion, in fact, is an ethical outlook bolstered up with 'stories'.

I have chosen to mention this particular attempt to deal with religious statements because it is typical as well as skilful. Its typicality consists in trying to show that metaphysical statements, statements about the supernatural are other than they appear: in particular, that they cannot be regarded as genuinely informative. This in itself is not a misconceived attempt: plenty of statements are not what they appear. But it is necessary to be very careful in assigning statements to classes in this way; and I do not think that writers of this kind have always kept a firm grasp of certain necessary points in connection with the use of language.

The most important of these is the point that it is primarily people who mean, and not statements. Language does not exist in the abstract, but is used by people with certain intentions, who desire to communicate. The appropriate question, therefore, is really not 'What does such-and-such a statement mean?' but 'What does so-and-so mean by this statement?' The same point applies to verification: we should ask not 'How is this statement verified?' but 'How do people who make this statement verify it?' This point may seem trivial. But to appreciate it entails appreciating that we may get different answers to our questions. It is easy to assume that statements have single meanings and single methods of verification; and though this may be generally true of other informative statements, it may not be true of metaphysical statements. Indeed, the answers which are given to a question about the meaning of a religious belief show a remarkable variety of opinion, even amongst those who share a common religion.

It would be erroneous to suppose, therefore, that because there is no standard meaning or verification for religious statements they are meaningless and unverifiable. Nearly all philosophers today admit that they are meaningful; indeed, it was never possible to hold that they were meaningless without adopting a monopolistic and unfairly restricted sense of 'meaning'. But it is an equal mistake to suppose that because all religious believers are not agreed upon what is to count as evidence for the truth of their statements, therefore nothing counts or could ever count. It may not be at all clear how these statements are to be verified or falsified, but this does not entail that they are not verifiable or falsifiable in principle. Neither does it entail that they are not informative.

In other words, the religious believer may meet the cross-questioning of the philosopher with a straight *nolle prosequi*. He may say simply, 'This statement is intended by me as informative.' The philosopher cannot sensibly reply, 'No, it's not.' He may point to a lack of agreed meaning and verification, show that most if not all other informative statements have agreed meaning and verification, and so on, but he cannot deny the speaker's intention: and he cannot show that the intention cannot in principle be fulfilled. For it may be possible to provide meaning and verification for the statement, or to agree on them. What the philosopher can try to do, however, is to show that whatever the intentions of the speaker, the statement is not actually informative. He will try to do this by showing that being informative, in the case of all statements, depends on the existence of agreed verification.

The religious believer is here faced with two alternatives. He can either say that his statements are not, after all, informative, thereby evading the attack altogether: or say that established meaning and verification is not in fact necessary for informative statements, thereby standing up to it. This is the crux of the matter, the rock which all metaphysics and religious belief must either escape or be wrecked on. And it seems to me tragic that religious believers do not realise that neither of the two alternatives I have mentioned are at all satisfactory.

First, the attempt to evade the attack. The attempt must fail, because it is these allegedly informative assertions which give to any religion its importance and its distinctive character. Statements which lay down language-rules ('A sacrament is an outward and visible sign of an inward and spiritual grace'), historical statements ('The man Jesus Christ was crucified in Palestine during the reign of Tiberius'), exhortations ('Brethren, let us love one another'), and moral injunctions ('Judge not'), all have obvious uses; but they would, none of them, have any peculiarly religious interest unless backed by a number of assertions about the supernatural. Thus, we are only interested in defining 'sacrament' clearly because it is held that the Son of God instituted certain sacraments: historical statements about

Jesus concern us only because we believe certain meta-physical statements about Him: and exhortations and in-junctions have religious force only because they derive from supernatural fact — hence we see arguments like: 'Let us love one another, for love is of God.' Most Christians, except under philosophical cross-examination, would surely regard the 'good news' of the Gospel as factually informative. To say 'There is a God' is to state a fact: God is real in the same *sense*, though not in the same way, as physical objects are real[1]: and the information which religious beliefs contain is not only supposed to be genuine, but of the utmost importance in the conduct of our lives.

The second alternative, that of claiming that statements can be informative without being verifiable in the sense required by philosophers, is more difficult to prove unsatisfactory. To begin with, many believers would hold that there was evidence for their beliefs. For some Christians, for instance, the supposed majesty and order of the natural universe is a proof of God's existence: to others, the life and personality of Christ is verification for His divinity: and so on. They might also admit that certain things counted against their beliefs: that the existence of pain and evil, for instance, counted against their belief in a loving and omnipotent God. Why is it, then, that philosophers still wish to insist that religious statements may not be verifiable? What precisely is this test of verification which they claim that all informative statements must pass?

The philosopher's point may be better made (as one or two philosophers have themselves suggested) in terms of

[1] This point is of central importance to my thesis: I have tried to expand and elucidate it on pp. 13-14.

falsification rather than verification; and the principle may be stated thus: 'If a statement is not decisively falsifiable, in principle as well as in practice, then the statement is not informative.' Of course this statement is itself somewhat vague: we may wonder what the phrase 'in principle' means, for instance. But the reasons for making it are tolerably clear. If you are trying to tell somebody that something is the case, this logically excludes certain other things being the case. For example, suppose I say, 'There is a tiger in the room.' Asked what evidence there was for this statement, or how it could be verified, I should mention pieces of evidence like there being a growling noise, a large striped animal with teeth and four legs, and so on. To say 'there is a tiger' entails there being a large striped animal, etc., because they are part of the meaning of the statement. The statement is vacuous without them. 'There is a tiger' is only informative if there is actually a large striped animal. Consequently, it must be decisively falsifiable: falsifiable, that is, if the pieces of evidence could not be found. Of course, the absence of only some of the evidence would not falsify it decisively: the growl might be absent, for instance, and there might still be a tiger. But there comes a time when the absence of evidence is overwhelming. An animal with three legs and no growl might still be a tiger; but an animal with no legs at all and a trunk could not be.

Moreover, statements are informative to the same degree as they are falsifiable or vulnerable. For the more precise information they give, the easier it is to upset them. 'There is something in the room' is very uninformative and not very vulnerable: 'there is an animal in the room' slightly more informative, but *ipso facto* more vulnerable: because more criteria have to be satisfied for 'animal' than for 'something'— the statement has to pass more verification-tests. 'There is a six-foot tiger exactly in the middle of the room, possessing only four teeth and pointing its tail consistently at an angle of seventy-eight degrees' is very precise, and very vulnerable. To put this more generally, any informative statement specifies that a part of reality is such-and-such: and the more precise the specification — the more the specification specifies, so to speak — then the more things there might be wrong with it.

If, then, a statement's truth is consistent with any evidence that might be forthcoming, it cannot be at all informative. Making a statement of this kind would be like saying: 'There is a tiger in the room, and nothing could count as evidence which decisively falsifies this truth.' Of course if there actually is a tiger, then the statement cannot actually be decisively falsified: for it is true. But it is still decisively falsifiable as a statement: for there is no logical compulsion about its being true. To say 'nothing could count as evidence against the existence of God' might mean 'since God exists, there can be no decisive evidence against it': but it might also mean that the statement 'God exists' is logically exempt from decisive evidence against it. And if this is true, then it cannot be informative. For saying 'God exists' is a particular instance of saying 'Such-and-such is the case'; and it is always logically possible that such-and-such is not the case. Whether it is or not precisely constitutes the test which any informative statement must pass.

Since therefore neither of these two alternatives is satisfactory, religious believers have to face up to the problem of providing their religious statements with established meaning and verification. In view of the points mentioned, they should be anxious rather than unwilling to make it clear what would decisively falsify the statements, since their informativeness corresponds to their falsifiability. Just how this process of giving verification to religious statements is to be gone through, I shall endeavour to explain in the next essay. So far as we are here concerned, the point I wish to establish is that our fifth class of statements — those apparently informative about the supernatural world — must be claimed as genuinely informative, with all that this implies. If they are to be merged with any other class, it must be with the third: those expressing factual truths, or what are generally known as empirical statements.

Providing statements with verification, however, is not an arbitrary process; and there is one further point which must be allowed to the philosopher. Informative statements inform us about something in our experience, and must therefore be verifiable ultimately by our experience. I do not mean, of course, that they are about something which we are actually touching, seeing, feeling, etc., or which we have touched, seen, felt, etc. 'There is a tiger in the room' is informative even though we may never have seen a tiger. But they must be about something of which we could in principle have experience: for if they were not, they would not inform us about anything at all which had any connection with our lives and interests. To say 'There is a tiger in the room' would be senseless, and certainly not informative, if I added 'but nobody could ever have any experience of such a thing'. The whole interest of making such a statement is that, if we enter the room, we can expect to experience certain things — growls, stripes, being eaten, and so on. Statements which are of public interest and are informative, like this one, are based on the experiences of some people, and on the possibility that other people may also have similar experiences. This is the purpose of informative communication.

Past writers have attempted to discover many loopholes which might enable them to avoid this point also; and it is impossible to demonstrate that all of them are culs-de-sac. A typical loophole is to say that God 'transcends' human experience, and that therefore we cannot expect to verify statements about God by human experience; though of course the first of these two statements need not be understood in such a way that the second follows from it. But the same dilemma presents itself. Either 'God' stands for something at least partly within our experience, so that statements with the word 'God' in them are to that extent experimentally verifiable: or else 'God' does not stand for something within our actual or potential experience, in which case (to put it bluntly) statements about God can have no possible interest for us, and may well be meaningless. Of course this dilemma could be put more forcibly. We could say that if a descriptive word is supposed to refer to something which could not be experienced, then it seems doubtful whether it describes anything at all: since to be a thing involves the capability of being experienced, and can only be known through experience.

Nor need the Christian attempt to take evasive action over the issue of verification in any other way. Philoso-

phers have been concerned to clarify the logical characteristics of informative assertions by various observations.
They have said that they must be meaningful and verifiable: that we must know what would count as evidence
for or against them: that their verification must ultimately
be conducted by somebody's experience: that unless these
conditions were satisfied they could not qualify for truth
or falsehood, and so on. All this can be accepted; and there
seems little use in trying to break out of the circle of these
observations at any point, e.g. by saying that Christian
assertions are 'true' in the sense of 'illuminating', or can be
'verified' 'by the Christian way of life itself.' For though
the points being made here may be valid and important,
they are insufficient; because Christian assertions are also
supposed, by Christians themselves, to be true and verifiable in the (possibly more usual) sense in which philosophers have used these words.

This attempt to put religious assertions in the same
logical boat, as it were, with straightforward empirical
statements looks naïve and old-fashioned, because it suggests a naïve and old-fashioned view of religious language.
We are accustomed to regard religious language as inadequate for its purposes; in particular, it is said to be 'metaphor' or 'analogy'. When challenged at every point, the
metaphor becomes 'eroded' or 'evaporates', until nothing
may be left. Hence the Christian and the philosopher
seem both driven to the view that the metaphorical assertions cannot be informative, and must be in a different
logical category from empirical statements, with a different
sort of meaning and verification, if indeed they have any
verification at all. But this is deceptive; because a metaphor

may assert something quite as precise and informative as any other assertion. A word used metaphorically or analogically may lose something of its straightforward meaning; but it may gain some other significance. For example, 'sugar is sweet' may be a straightforward empirical assertion, and 'Mary is sweet' a metaphor; but it would be wrong to suppose that what we are saying about Mary is less definite or meaningful than what we are saying about sugar. The word 'sweet' simply means different things, and has a different method of verification, in either case. This might well be true of religious assertions. They are expressed in language borrowed from non-religious contexts, just as 'Mary is sweet' uses a word borrowed from taste-experience; but this language may well have a new and precise significance, though of course the fact that the same word is used suggests that there are points of contact between the two uses — points which might help to make the new use more comprehensible to someone who did not understand the metaphorical meaning.

One essential task which religious believers have to perform, therefore, is to give the individual words in religious language a clear and unambiguous descriptive meaning where such meaning is required. This applies both to what we might call technical religious words — words like 'God', 'soul', 'grace', and so on — and also to words used metaphorically — 'love', 'father', 'kingdom', etc. Hitherto many believers have clung desperately to these words, but have been more able to say what they do not mean than what they do. Yet if religious language is ever to be genuinely and importantly informative, it is important that the criteria for the use of these words should be clear. If this task is not achieved, we shall be reduced to saying, as the Vedantist says when asked to describe his deity, 'Not this, not this'.

To many people this might seem to imply that God is an object, much like a table or an elephant, Who can be immediately and wholly comprehended by experience: the only slight difference being that a different kind of experience is required. Yet this is plainly absurd; and a God of this kind is not the sort of God in which anybody believes. But we must be careful to understand the point. I have said earlier in this chapter that God is real in the same sense, though not in the same way, that physical objects are real. He must be real in the same sense: for the word 'real' has, in fact, only one sense — either something is real and exists, or it is unreal and does not exist. 'Real' and 'exists' are definitely not ambiguous words. But He is not (putting it roughly) real in the same *way*, because He is not the same sort of thing as a table or an elephant: indeed, we might say that He is not a *thing* at all, and certainly that He is not an object. Briefly, then, my contention is that if God is real and exists, the unambiguous logic and language of statements about existence, and the verification needed for these statements, must apply to God as much as to anything else, for these are part and parcel of what we mean by words like 'exist' and 'real'; but this is not to deny that much of His nature may be mysterious and uncomprehended by men. In much the same way, we might hold that love, or Martians, or the fourth dimension exist and are real: we might be able to give these words and phrases clear and unambiguous descriptive meanings and verification-methods: but they might still be very different from other things, highly mysterious, and largely uncomprehended.

Instead of the Vedantist's 'Not this, not this', Christians must be able to say, 'At least this, and at least this.' They must be able to assert definitely about God, whilst admitting that there is far more to be known about Him than we can perhaps ever hope to know. Moreover, as we come to learn more about God, there is nothing in logic to prevent our expanding the meaning of the word 'God'. In just such a way the word 'desire' has, since Freudian psychology, become expanded to include the concept of unconscious desires. In the light of new experience, words change their meaning in order to incorporate and communicate the experience. A due observance of logic, therefore, does nothing to remove the mystery of God on which Christians rightly insist; but it does serve the useful purpose of reminding us that if we are to talk meaningfully about God at any particular time, we must know what the word 'God' is agreed to mean at that time, and that we can ultimately know this only by reference to experience.

Another and equally important task for believers is to adopt a firm and unambiguous classification of the statements and sentences in their religion. Much that is spoken and written about religion is vitiated by the absence of such a classification; and it is particularly difficult for non-believers to achieve a firm grasp of the logical structure of religious doctrine. It is annoying, for instance, to argue at length about whether the soul is immortal, only to find after a time that the word 'soul' is being used to mean 'the immortal part of man'. This of course makes the statement 'The soul is immortal' analytic or tautologous, and therefore not empirically informative. In trying to assess the truth of a complex metaphysical system, such as the doctrines of the Roman church, it is essential to be clear about which statements are supposed to be informative and verifiable, and which are supposed to follow by deductive argument from other statements. For example, if we were intended to accept a number of statements on the authority of Christ, the Bible, the Church or some other source, we should be particularly interested in verifying the statements which were relevant to showing that source to be reliable, and not waste time in examining the statements deduced from its reliability.

This task of establishing meaning and verification, and classifying statements in religious belief according to their logic, has hardly been started. Hitherto Christian apologists have been chiefly interested in trying to collect and assess evidence for their beliefs, not realising the importance of the (logically prior) question of what is to count as evidence. Until this question is settled, it is unlikely that many people will be convinced by this collected 'evidence': for it may not be evidence to them at all. One cannot tell whether something is evidence for a statement or not unless one first knows what sort of statement it is supposed to be, and what sorts of things count as evidence for it. And it is this lack of clarity, if I may be permitted to conclude with a sociological sidelight, which has engendered a situation in which many intelligent people are now neither convinced of, nor hostile to, Christian belief, but merely uninterested in it.

2

Religious Experience[1]

I shall now try to answer the fundamental challenge represented by the question, 'How are religious statements ultimately verified?' Briefly, my answer will be 'By religious experience': though there is much ground to be covered before we can regard that answer as philosophically satisfactory. I begin by assuming, as we saw in the last essay, that religious statements are supposed to be factually informative, like empirical statements: that when we talk of 'God', we intend to refer to something that really exists. I wish to make one more assumption: namely, that there is such a thing as religious experience. I do not wish to say that it is genuine, in the sense that it is experience *of* anything: that would make the argument circular. Neither do I wish to investigate its psychological or other causes, which would be philosophically irrelevant. I mean only, what few would surely deny, that there is such a thing as mystical or religious experience: that those who have such experience are not lying when they say that they have it.

Let it be granted, then, that some people have experiences which seem to them different in kind from any other type of experience, and that they propose to base certain assertions on these experiences. These assertions

[1] This chapter is printed in a larger and slightly modified form in *The Hibbert Journal*.

are supposed to be existential, in the sense that 'there is a G d' is supposed to be like 'There are tables' rather than 'I feel happy', and 'God is love' like 'The sky is blue' rather than 'I seem to see a blue patch'. We may put precisely the same point by saying that these experiences are supposed to be cognitive: they are supposed to be experiences *of* something. We may even say, if we like, that they are meant to be 'objective' rather than 'subjective', provided we do not mislead ourselves by these words. The root of the problem, therefore, consists in determining the minimum conditions necessary for the basing of existential assertions on experience, or for regarding experiences as cognitive. The phrase 'minimum necessary conditions' is important, because I do not want to hold at all that religious assertions are so firmly based on experience as ordinary empirical assertions. There are many sufficient conditions satisfied by empirical assertions which religious assertions do not satisfy. I wish only to claim that religious assertions can satisfy all the necessary ones.

There are several conditions which are certainly sufficient, but which are not necessary. In order to show this, we have only to construct logically possible cases where we would want to say that assertions of fact or existential assertions were being made, but where these conditions are not satisfied.

(*a*) Ability to make scientific tests of our experience is not necessary. Thus, we would be (and in fact have been) convinced that the sky was blue and the grass green without being able to measure light-waves or assess refraction. Though it may be necessary that there should be some kind of public test for an existential assertion, it is not necessary that the test should be sophisticated.

(*b*) It is not necessary that the experience should be shared by a majority of people: this is not a question of counting heads. If a majority of people were colour-blind, we should still accept existential statements about colours; and though a majority of people may not be able to hear the squeak of bats, we should still be prepared to believe that bats squeak.

(*c*) It is not necessary that the experience should be, as it were, presented to us on a plate, whole and complete. It may be true of an experience both that it is cognitive, and that we have to learn how to have it. This has occurred in the life-history of all of us, for all infants have to learn how to use their senses: just as men who are born blind and recover their sight have to learn how to use their eyes.

(*d*) It is not necessary that the testing-system for assertions should be universally adopted, or that the terms figuring in the assertions should have a meaning constant for all groups of people who make them. Thus, we can imagine different ways of testing for colour in different groups of people (by simply looking at colours, by matching them, by trying them in different lights, by scientific measurement, and so on). The only common factor would be that the tests involved something which one saw — that they referred to one particular type of experience: the actual tests and methods involved might differ widely. Similarly, the meanings of colour-words differ from one society to another: Latin and Greek colour-words are notoriously unlike our own.

(*e*) Finally, it is often said that if an assertion is existential and true, it must afford one the ability to predict. Thus, 'I seem to see a blue expanse' allows no important prediction: but 'the sky is blue now' allows one to predict that (other things being equal) the sun will be shining outside, the weather will be right for a picnic, and so on. But we must be careful how far we extend the notion of prediction here. Prediction of a sophisticated or scientific nature — or any prediction beyond what is implied by the assertion itself — is not a necessary condition. Thus if I say 'there is a table in the next room', and you are assured of the truth of this, we may say, if we like, that you are hence able to predict that if you go into the next room you will see something solid, probably with legs, with a flat top, on which you can put things, and so on. But all this is part of what we normally mean by 'table': it is implied in the assertion itself. When I say 'there is a table' I imply that if you do certain things, you will have certain experiences: in other words, that the statement is verifiable. It is not necessary that you should be able to use my statement to 'predict' in any wider sense. We can even imagine a society which did not use its experiences of colour to predict in any but this narrow sense: a society which never connected black clouds with rain, or blue skies with sunshine, or red rags with bulls charging. To put this point in the least misleading way I can think of, it is not necessary to predict that anything will happen, though it is necessary to predict that we will be able to have certain experiences.

In what, then, does the difference between existential and non-existential ('psychological') statements consist? It is sometimes said that the former are 'corrigible' and the latter 'incorrigible'. But this will certainly not do as it stands. Statements like 'I feel happy' and 'I feel pain' are corrigible by other people. Even if we discount the possibility that I may be lying, or that I am not using the right words to describe my experience, there still remain tests which can be made by an outsider. If you assert that you feel happy, you may not be lying, but you may be deceiving yourself. That is why, if someone asks, 'Do you feel happy?' one often takes a long time to consider one's answer. The outsider can check one's answer, to some extent at least, by observing one's behaviour. If I scowl and look sullen, have frequent quarrels with my wife and detest my work, most people would agree that I was not feeling happy; but it is quite possible for me to believe the opposite. All that remains of the 'corrigible' and 'incorrigible' distinction, I think, is that if I am asserting something solely about my own experiences (and am neither a liar nor ignorant of common usage), then nobody else is likely to be in a position to refute me. There is an obvious sense in which nobody else can have my experiences. But many 'psychological' statements, like 'I feel happy' and 'I feel pain', entail far more than a verbal echo of simple experiences; and for that reason they are verifiable by other people.

This point is not essential to my case, since I should want to say, of course, that religious assertions are corrigible, and that religious experience may not be genuine (in the sense that it may not be cognitive experience). But it serves to bring out what I take to be the real difference between existential and non-existential statements, which is that the former are concerned with matters of public interest and experience to a degree that the latter are not. For example: suppose I say, in the first place, 'I feel great pain.' This is a non-existential assertion, and nobody would take exception to it. But suppose I then say, archaically, 'There is a great pain within me.' This looks like an existential assertion. If we attack this second assertion, it becomes apparent in the course of time that what I am saying refers only, or at least very largely, to my own experiences, and neither the actual or potential experiences of other people. It says nothing more than 'I feel great pain'; and it would lose nothing by adopting this, rather than the existential, form of speech. 'There is a table in the next room', on the other hand, does assert something of public interest, in the sense that it is verifiable by public experience to a far higher degree than psychological assertions.

We use these two modes of speech, existential and psychological, precisely because we wish to distinguish matters which are of public interest from matters which are not: to distinguish autobiographical remarks from common facts. Roughly, we begin thinking and talking in terms of existence or non-existence, in terms of objects or 'realities', in all cases where the experience of a sufficient number of people is coincidental: this is the easiest way of communicating our experiences to each other. I say 'There is a table': by this you are led to expect certain experiences of your own. Confident expectations of this kind are convenient to us.

We must remember, however, that if we want to talk about cognitive experience, or 'what is really there', our very language implies the possibility of non-cognitive experience in the same field, or 'what isn't really there', i.e. illusions. This implies that there must be certain tests for distinguishing reality from illusion, cognitive experience from non-cognitive, and what is really there from what is not. This is an important point, and must be met by anyone who proposes to establish any kind of object-language. Phrases like 'a sixth sense', 'something which we experience' (using 'experience' transitively), 'supernatural reality' and so on do not carry their own guarantee. But granted at least the possibility of such tests, it is not at all clear what could be meant by asking whether a whole *type* of experience is cognitive or not.

This question seems academic, in that it rests upon a misunderstanding of language. Suppose I say, 'There is an elephant in the next room.' You say, 'What do you mean by that?' I reply, 'Well, most of what I mean is that if you and other people were to enter the room, you would have such-and-such sense-experiences.' You check whether these experiences are actually to be had, and find that they are. But you are not content: you say, perhaps, 'Yes, you are right about the experiences; but surely this does not entitle you to make any existential statement: they might be "subjective", or self-induced, or non-cognitive.' Then I say: 'Well, I think I can convince you that they are not illusory: I know no scientific tests, but you will find that a large number of people have the experiences, and that they are not drunk, or subject to illusions, or liars.' You say, 'Perhaps so; but I still do not see that any number of experiences entitles you to make this existential assertion.' Then I begin to lose patience: I say, 'My dear fellow, I am no philosopher: if you don't want to call my statement "existential", then don't. All I really mean to assert is included in the experiences which you have already admitted: this is what I mean by "There is an elephant". I can't understand what you mean by asking for proof that the experiences are cognitive, or that the existential statement is justified, or that the elephant is "really" there.'

This is the point which is surely of the greatest practical importance in discussions between believers and non-believers: it comes out more clearly, perhaps, when it is not being argued by philosophers than when it is. A says: 'There is a God.' B says: 'How do you know?' A says: 'I have had certain experiences: I have seen God, talked with Him, been a changed man ever since, etc.' But this is of merely psychological or autobiographical interest to B: what B wants to know is whether there 'really' is a God, or whether A is just a dreamer. And the whole question is whether the experiences which A uses to base his assertion upon are available to B also. If they are, or even if there is any possibility of their being, then B will be interested: we have now stopped being autobiographical, and begun to deal with matters of common experience or potential experience. B will then want to know how he can have these experiences: in other words, he will want to verify and make tests for A's assertion.

A's assertion, in my view, is existential at least in the sense that it is supposed to be publicly verifiable, and that there are supposed to be tests for it. But I should want to say more than this. I should want to say that there are groups — large groups — of religious believers who do use the same system of verification for religious assertions, by means of their common experiences. These experiences are not only common (i.e. shared by all of them), but they are also co-recurrent. By this I mean that a number of numerically different experiences recur together in the same contexts. Further, having one or more of these experiences enables them to expect or predict other experiences. For instance, supposing a believer has experiences of love, grace and power, he can predict the result of a further test, e.g. what will happen if he prays, or confesses his sins. (Of course these words are technical terms to believers; if they worry non-believers we can say that experiences e, f and g allow one to predict experiences h and i.) This seems to me precisely similar in point of logic to the case with assertions like 'There is a table'. My having had certain visual experiences (seen a table) enables me to predict other experiences (touching it, putting things on it, etc.).

Religious assertions, then, do concern matters of public interest, at least within the religious groups who use the same verification-system for their assertions. They are publicly verifiable at least to a limited public. This means that there are ways of distinguishing genuine from misleading religious experience. It is admittedly unfortunate that some Christian writers should have spoken as if any kind of experience that might be labelled 'religious' or 'mystical' somehow carried its own guarantee. In fact, of course, most Christians would surely want to say that some religious believers — the worshippers of Baal, for instance — did have religious or ecstatic experiences which were not genuine or misleading: misleading, because they based on them assertions about God which were not true. Within the Christian group 'God' entails the possibility of a number of experiences (love, grace, power). If a man has only one of these, he may find it deceptive, in exactly the same way as if a man only experiences dagger-like visual images, he may find these to be unsubstantiated by the other experiences which must be available if there is really a dagger there. Further tests will show whether the single experience is deceptive or genuine.

Does this mean that religious assertions cannot be understood by those who have no religious experiences? The answer to this depends upon what is to count as understanding. In what seems to me the most important sense, religious assertions can be understood. Believers can define the terms of such assertions in terms of actual or potential experiences for the benefit of non-believers, just as a man with normal eyesight can explain the meaning of 'table' in terms of visual experiences to a blind man. An unbeliever can know what 'God' means, just as a blind man can know what 'table' means; that is, both can know how and when to use these words, what conditions must be satisfied before they can be used correctly. But in what is also an important sense, a man who has not had or cannot have any kind of experience of the *type* relevant to an assertion cannot understand the assertion. Explaining religious assertions to a non-believer is not at all like explaining the meaning of 'table' to someone who has never seen a table, but who has the use of his eyes. For here we can draw parallels: we can say, perhaps, 'Imagine something square, with legs, elevated from the ground, etc.' He would be able to appreciate the kind of experiences relevant to assertions about tables: the experiences, we might say, which make up the component parts of 'table'. It is much more like trying to explain empirical assertions to an extra-terrestrial race of people who have no sense experiences at all. One could acquaint them with definitions and verification-tests, but one would get no further. Nothing one could say would seem real to them, until they were able to have at least some sense experiences.

I have avoided bringing in the debatable parallel with 'aesthetic experience' hitherto; but it is worth mentioning at this point, if only for purposes of illustration. For here too (a) we can make no scientific tests: (b) many aesthetic experiences are not shared by a majority of people: (c) it is often necessary to learn to have this experience ('musical appreciation' classes): (d) there is no universally adopted testing system for statements about works of art, and different terms ('romantic', 'baroque', etc.) have different meanings for different groups: (e) no sophisticated prediction is possible from these statements, but prediction about aesthetic experiences entailed by the statements is possible. Thus, if I say, 'Beethoven's "Eroica" is noble, dramatic and powerful,' you are entitled to assume that if you make the appropriate tests you will have certain experiences.

Tests in aesthetic experience also bear a remarkable resemblance to tests in religious experience. Neither consist in using the senses alone, or in measuring, observing, counting, etc.: we should not expect this, of course, since the statements are not intended to refer to objects or qualities of sense experience. Yet it is possible to test 'Beethoven's "Eroica" is noble'. I can acquaint myself with Beethoven's music in general, rid myself of prejudice for or against Beethoven, and above all simply listen to the 'Eroica' on many occasions over a long period of time. Religious tests have a good deal in common with this. We are told to clear the mind of prejudice, acquaint ourselves with religion in general, attempt to disregard sense experience for the moment, contemplate, meditate, and so on.

Again, we can admit ourselves mistaken about aesthetic merit. We can say, 'I thought so-and-so was a very powerful composer when I was young, but now I see that most of his work is mere bombast,' implying thereby that the tests we made when young were inadequate in some way. Similarly we can say, 'There seems to be something great about this work,' or 'There is something great about this work': and these have different meanings. We say the first, perhaps, when we have only heard it once — when we have not conducted enough tests to be sure. As with empirical statements, we preserve a distinction between autobiographical or psychological remarks ('I like this', 'This moves me greatly'), and assertions ('This is great music', 'That is a really beautiful passage').

Finally, it is noticeable that within a group whose members have common aesthetic experiences sensible and meaningful (and often helpful) conversations may be conducted which (in one sense) may be nonsense to outsiders. The group might make it plain to an outsider that when they used a word ('romantic') they referred to various aesthetic experiences (strangeness, poignancy), so that the outsider could know what the word meant; but the conversation could hardly be real to him. This frequently happens in religion also. Religious people often appear to be arguing about assertions in a way which seems quite unreal to a non-believer; and this is perfectly understandable, just as it is understandable that a discussion about music should make no sense to a man who was tone-deaf.

Both aesthetic and religious assertions refer to potential experiences, experiences which are actual within certain groups. It may be true that these experiences could become actual for a vast majority of people: that the capacity for religious experience has for some reason become repressed in modern societies. But I do not think that very much turns on this question in point of logic, though it does in point of practice. I am more concerned to discover what our attitude should be towards religious assertions. As things are, we have groups who claim to have certain experiences, on which they base verification-systems and existential assertions. What would be a rational attitude for someone who did not have these experiences?

Suppose a group of people were to lay claim to unusual experiences on which they based assertions that certain things called squmps existed. We should first want to know whether the existence of squmps was verifiable by any normal method — by sense experience, for instance. But no, this is not the case: a different type of experience is involved. Squmps have no connections with the natural world, at least in this direct way. We should then want to know whether these experiences had been properly formulated into a language-system which distinguished psychological from existential statements. Yes, this is so: it is possible for a member of the group to say 'I thought I saw a sqump yesterday, but it wasn't one', or 'That seems like a sqump, but I'm not sure', and also, 'That's definitely a sqump, it passes all the tests of experience.' At this point we must surely admit that there are existential statements about squmps. Then, surely, we should want to know just how important the whole matter was. Is there any purpose in having experiences of squmps? Or can we just shrug our shoulders when people start talking about them? In particular, if squmps are important — perhaps they illuminate our moral problems, or give us a feeling of beauty or security — can we learn to experience them?

Here, of course, the religious believer will answer with a definite 'Yes'. (It is worth noticing that the music-lover can also say 'Yes'; he can say that if you make no attempt to appreciate music, you will be missing a lot, and that once you appreciate it sufficiently, you will find it convenient to make assertions about it.) Christians at least suppose everyone to be capable of religious experience ('knowing God'), and believe it to be of immense importance and benefit to the lives of all men. Both these suppositions may be true; and it seems to me that the most rational course is to try to find out, not to shrug one's shoulders.

What we can legitimately demand of religious believers is that they should try to put forward some sort of unanimous programme for the benefit of those who want to have these experiences and test the assertions based on them. There are certain features common to the tests used by most religious groups, but it would help enormously if non-believers could be presented with a single programme. In this religion has hitherto failed; and this, together with all the other disadvantages which pertain to religious assertions as compared with assertions about sense experience, which I have described above, has made a great many people despair of ever founding religious belief on a secure logical and epistemological basis. This despair is natural but unnecessary. None of the disadvantages are fatal, and the difficulties which lie in our way are difficulties of practice, and not of logic.

It may well be asked why, if all this is acceptable, religious believers have not taken this line more clearly. But there are plenty of reasons for this. First, many believers have (mistakenly) demanded logical certainty for their assertions of fact. Secondly, their own religious experience, though sufficient for assertions, is more uncertain and fluctuating than sense experience, so that they have preferred to base their assertions on some other (illegitimate) foundation. Thirdly, they have not noticed the differences of language- and verification-systems between different religious groups. Fourthly, the structure of religious belief is not always clearly demonstrated by believers, although it is usually evident that a great many assertions may not be directly verifiable by experience, but depend logically on others: for instance, if we could verify by experience that there was a God, and that Christ always said what was true about Him, and that Christ asserted such-and-such, then we should be entitled to believe a great many other assertions. We might add to these points the desire of many believers to convert and propagandise by methods which are irrational and logically illegitimate: centuries of tradition and evangelistic zeal do not assist unbiased philosophical consideration.

All this, of course, does not mean that all or any religious assertions are actually true: this is not a philosophical question. But it does mean, I think, that they have a chance of being true along the lines suggested. What is required above all is that believers should present a solid front, at least on those assertions about which they agree. They should be able to put forward a clear and unanimous programme, describing some approved method of obtaining the experiences which are relevant to the key assertions of their faith. Whether they can learn anything from the mystics, from Wordsworth, from Mr. Huxley or from anyone else I do not know. But until they lay down some sort of agreed tests for their assertions, by means of religious experience, I do not see how they can expect anyone to place rational belief in them. What we need here, I take it, is a combination of mystic and of analytical philosopher. Perhaps this is too much to ask.

3

Authority and Belief

Most Christians, if asked why they held certain metaphysical beliefs, would not reply by quoting intellectual arguments or by bringing forward subtle evidence. They would base their acceptance of the beliefs on their acceptance of an authority. This authority may be, for example, their Church or their Bible: ultimately, however, it is likely to be the person of Christ Himself. 'I believe it to be true because Christ said so' is a common reply. This fits in very well with what we are often told about the Christian faith: namely, that it is not primarily the acceptance of metaphysical doctrine but the acceptance of a person. It seems plausible to hope, therefore, for a rational defence of Christian doctrine in terms of Christ's authority.

It is, of course, only reasonable to rely upon an authority if we have reason to believe that the authority is reliable; and the question therefore turns simply on whether Christians can reasonably claim that Christ is such an authority. In connection with this it is important to notice that the emotional effect or personal impact which a man may have upon us, whatever sort of effect or impact it may be, is not in itself evidence of his reliability. Experiences of this kind are not self-guaranteeing. The mere power of Christ's appeal, therefore, is not sufficient for our purpose. We need to show that He is a reliable authority on matters of doctrine and metaphysics: and for this we require more objective evidence.

It is important to make some distinction between believing in a person and believing that a statement which he makes is true. This distinction holds even when we believe statements to be true on authority. To say that you believe in a man usually means that you trust him or rely on him in certain respects, generally specified by the context. Thus one might say, having picked an unlikely-looking candidate for an important post, 'I believe in him,' meaning that you rely on his doing the job well and have confidence in his ability to do it well. We could perhaps distinguish two elements in 'believing in' somebody: first, a belief that he will behave in certain ways, and secondly, a feeling of confidence that goes with the belief. Thus, if you choose a guide when you are lost and believe in him, you believe that he is likely to lead you in the right direction, and you place your trust in him. The first represents an opinion about what is true or probable, and the second a psychological attitude. Believing a statement to be true, however, does not necessarily involve a psychological attitude of this kind. Certainly belief in statements does entail some sort of psychological attitude towards them: but the attitudes which we adopt towards statements are not the same as those which we adopt towards people.

Believing in someone, like all other attitudes, is of course only rational when there are reasons why we should believe in him; this is a near-tautology. To say 'I have no reason to believe in Smith, but I do believe in him' does not repre-

D

sent a rational attitude. Certainly, the reasons for believing in somebody need not be easily stated or overwhelming: the belief of a mother that her son has not committed a crime, when all the apparent evidence is against him, may be quite rational: for she has (or may have) access to valid evidence which cannot be produced in a court of law — her intimate and long-continued knowledge of her son. But there must be some reasons or some evidence, and the reasons or evidence must be relevant to the context of the belief.

We may 'believe in' Christ in many different ways. We may believe in Him as a guide in life, as a great ethical teacher, as a master psychologist, as a stranger who is fighting on our side, or as the divine and infallible Son of God. In all these cases we would place confidence in Him. But together with our confidence or faith, if our believing in Him is rational, will go a belief or beliefs that He will behave in certain ways: that He will guide us aright, teach us correctly about what is good, make our minds function healthily, actually fight on our side, or always act and speak divinely and infallibly. The evidence for these (propositional) beliefs will differ very much from case to case. But in some of the cases severe difficulties arise. For we have established evidence, and established means of testing, some of these beliefs, but not others. Thus it would be possible to hold that we have criteria for deciding whether or not a man is a good guide in life, a great ethical teacher, a master psychologist or a warrior who is fighting on our side: though even in some of these cases the criteria could be questioned. But what are the criteria for testing whether someone is the Son of God? We simply do not have any.

Nor is it likely that we shall have any until we have some sort of knowledge about God: whether He exists, what He is like, and so on. Without this, we can hardly quote rational evidence for our belief. Indeed, unless we know what 'X is the Son of God' means, and what would count as evidence for it, we cannot possibly know whether it is true at all.

We cannot, therefore, logically take belief *in* Christ as a divine authority as a starting-point for our religious beliefs generally. For if this belief is to be reasonable, we must also have reason to believe *that* something is the case: namely, that He is the Son of God. And it is precisely religious beliefs of this kind that present the greatest problems, simply because their use and logic is wholly unclear. Yet it might still seem possible to assent to certain of Christ's statements, including the statement that He is the Son of God, on the grounds that Christ is an authority on the truth of statements of this kind. All I have shown is that to argue that Christ is an authority because He is the Son of God is to argue in a circle.

To believe that a statement is true on authority, however, has difficulties of its own; and when the statement is in any degree questionable, this sort of belief is usually far more vulnerable than 'belief in' a person. For though belief in a person does involve belief that something is the case, we can usually verify the latter for ourselves. Thus, supposing I lend £5 to a man, and when questioned about whether he is to be trusted, say, 'I believe in him: it'll be all right.' This involves believing that the man is trustworthy. If I do believe this, it is probable that I myself have some evidence for it. Perhaps I have lent him money in the past, and he has never failed to repay it: or perhaps I know from experience that people of his type are always trustworthy. In any case, I do not have to rely upon an authority for my belief. It is the trusting of an authority for the truth of statements that generates the difficulties, and makes the belief more vulnerable.

We may list a number of criteria — not necessarily exhaustive — for belief on authority, where such belief is supposed to be rational:

1. The person whose authority we trust must be sincere: he must not be lying, or inspired by partisanship. If an eminent scientist tells us that Bloggs' pills cure all ills, it becomes definitely less reasonable to believe this when we learn that the scientist is employed by Bloggs to advertise his pills. He may either be lying, or allowing his loyalty to his employer to run away with him. In either case, and in all similar cases, his authority is suspect.

2. The person must actually be an authority, and not merely pose as one. Thus, we take with a pinch of salt a statement like 'All the Russians love their political system' if made by someone who has only spent three weeks in Russia.

3. The person must be speaking within his authority. Thus, a man may be an authority on astronomy and cosmology, and we listen to his statements about the universe, galaxies, nebulae, etc., with respect and confidence. But when he begins — often in the same breath, and without any indication of a change of subject — to talk about 'the hand of God' or 'the mind behind the matter' we may suspect that he has stopped talking science, and is talking

theology, in which he is not necessarily expert or authoritative. This is often very difficult to detect.

4. The field of knowledge in which the person works must be a genuine field, and must have genuine experts. Thus the statement, 'People born under the sign of Mars have fiery dispositions,' may be true, and is certainly verifiable; but we should not accept it on the authority of an astrologer unless we thought that there were authoritative astrologers: i.e. experts whose science gave them knowledge denied to ordinary people. This is different from (2): there are experts on Russia, but we may doubt whether there are experts on astrology.

5. The statement which the person makes must be meaningful and verifiable. This is not to say that we ourselves must know what it means or how to verify it. I could quite reasonably believe one of Einstein's equations ($E = Mc$ squared) without knowing what any of the terms meant. But this would only be reasonable because I have reason to believe that the equation is meaningful and verifiable: if not by me, then by Einstein and other mathematicians. In other words, the statement must fall in an established field of discourse and knowledge. If we have no reason to believe it meaningful and verifiable, then we have no reason to believe it true.

Of course we do believe a great many things on authority, and quite reasonably so. But it is worth noting that we are bound in the end to rely upon our own experience and our own reasoning, and that the more remote the statement from that experience, the more vulnerable our belief is likely to be. I believe that the English Channel is about

twenty miles wide, for instance; and this belief is well supported by different pieces of evidence of which I have first-
hand knowledge. I know that the geographical and carto-
graphical experts whom I trust are reliable, because they
make many statements of whose truth I have first-hand
experience. In the last resort, I could measure the width
of the Channel myself. But in believing that $E = Mc$
squared I am in a much more precarious position. I cannot
be sure, without placing a great deal of confidence in the
sincerity and ability of Einstein and other experts, that
this is a verifiable equation, or that Einstein is speaking
within his authority: though I may be more sure that
Einstein is not lying, that there are authorities on physics,
and that he is one.

It is to be noted that criteria (3) and (4) depend on (5).
We can tell whether a person is sincere and truthful, and
whether he has spent the necessary time and energy on a
subject to be authoritative, without necessarily knowing
that the subject is a genuine field of knowledge, that can
produce meaningful and verifiable statements. But we
cannot be sure of (3) — that he is speaking within his
authority — or of (4) — that the field of knowledge has
genuine experts — without being sure that the field of
knowledge is genuine: that there is really knowledge
available, not merely a number of statements which
have no established criteria of evidence, whose logic is
unclear.

These last criteria — particularly (5), but also (3) and
(4), which depend on (5) — are not satisfied by belief
in metaphysical statements which have the authority of
Christ; unless, of course, we have previously satisfied them

by other means. If we have already established a basis of meaning and verification for religious beliefs, no doubt we could satisfy the criteria; but this *ipso facto* precludes our taking Christ's authority as a starting-point. If we do not believe in the supernatural at all, we cannot be rationally persuaded by any such means as these. But that does not entail, either that it is unreasonable to believe *in* Christ, or that it is unreasonable to base a large part of our metaphysical doctrines on His teaching.

It may plausibly be asked; 'In what way is it possible to regard Christ as an expert at all?' Certainly He was no scientist. But to restrict the word 'expert' or 'authority' to scientific contexts would be monopolistic. The point is merely verbal: for it is plain that we might reasonably come to rely upon Christ, whether or not we care to call Him an expert. Precisely in what fields this reliability operates, however, is not altogether clear. It would be highly misleading to say that He could be relied on as an ethical or moral expert; for this would suggest that moral views were true and verifiable in the same sense that empirical and scientific statements are true and verifiable, which is not the case. A moral view cannot always be proved false by a consideration of facts: we may willingly concede all the excellent points made by modern philosophers in this connection.[1] Nevertheless, people plainly do rely upon Christ, and find their reliance justified.

Suppose that your end or objective in life, the way of life which you set out to follow, consists in the attainment of certain things which we may call roughly happiness, contentment, strength, integration, and so on. You then be-

[1] For a fuller discussion of the point see Chapter 7.

come acquainted with Christ, perhaps through the Bible: you read, 'Take my yoke upon you: for my yoke is easy, and my burden is light,' and various other passages suggesting that Christ will enable you to attain these objectives. You try out Christ's methods, in one or two instances, as a sort of test: you find that they work. In consequence you come to place reliance on those methods, just as you come to place reliance on a dictionary after testing its accuracy. You find that His way is satisfactory to you. All this is reasonable enough. We might prefer to say, perhaps, that His authority here is more like that of the psychologist than the moralist; but in any case, it is an authority that can be tested.

But this does not apply to His metaphysical teaching, since we have no means of testing the truth of metaphysical statements unless we have ourselves previously had experience of the supernatural, or have reason to believe that the supernatural exists. The two questions which the agnostic might ask here are (i) How do we know that there is a genuine field of knowledge of the supernatural at all? and (ii) How do we know that Christ is an expert in this field? These questions represent the criteria to which we have already drawn attention: and the criteria are necessary ones. Of the two, (i) is obviously the more radical. Indeed, it is unanswerable. For if we do know that we can make true statements about the supernatural, we have used something other than Christ's teaching as our starting-point: and if we do not know, then we cannot be sure that Christ's teaching is meaningful and verifiable — we have failed to satisfy the criterion. (ii) is somewhat easier: for once we do know how to verify metaphysical statements, we can easily test Christ's teaching and discover thereby whether we can reasonably regard Him as an authority.

It will be seen that this does not preclude believing in Christ as a guide in our moral and psychological life, as a friend, counsellor, source of strength, etc. Nor — once we have established tests for metaphysical statements, and hence indirectly for the reliability of metaphysicians — does it prevent us from accepting a large part of His teaching on trust, if we find by testing that it is trustworthy. I myself would base a good number of my beliefs on this principle. What it precludes is taking Christ's statements 'on trust' or 'on authority' without bothering about tests at all.

There is still a sense, however, in which Christ's statements may be used as the sole starting-point for metaphysical belief, though the starting-point is earlier than we might have thought at first. By following His advice we may be led to have experiences of the supernatural, on the basis of which we may come to believe that there is a genuine field of knowledge. From these experiences we may be able to establish meaning, verification and truth along the lines suggested in my last essay. If, for instance, we are led by Him to pray, worship, contemplate, and so on, we may find that we meet something that we should want to call, and could sensibly call, God: and we could construct a language to describe these meetings and experiences, which could yield true statements. Following His advice might even entail pretending to beliefs which it would otherwise be irrational to hold: e.g., we might assume the existence of God in order to discover whether we could have genuine experience of the supernatural in prayer or worship. This sort of pretence, undertaken simply for the purposes of trying to have certain experiences and make certain tests, is entirely reasonable. It could be compared with the sort of 'faith' or effort of belief which one tries to engender, for example, in people who are trying to discover the aesthetic qualities of great music. It is often helpful for such people to believe, or assume, that there are really certain experiences to be had from (say) Beethoven's symphonies, that these works are powerful, dramatic, poignant, and so on. If they fail to have the experiences, of course, they can retract their belief: just as we would legitimately retract our assumed belief in the supernatural if we and other people had failed to experience it, after using all reasonable methods. The rationality of this assumed belief — really little more than a make-believe — has a strictly pragmatic value: it helps us to make better tests. If we find that the tests are positive, that a judicious and representative selection of Christ's statements pass them, and that these results show Christ to be master of a knowledge of the supernatural far in advance of the ordinary person, then it would be reasonable to accept Him as an authority, and hence accept His teaching as authoritative.

In practice, however, I do not think that this method of arriving at religious truth is very likely to be successful: not because Christ's teaching is false or ineffectual, but because it was not directed at the sort of audience which we have been considering. Christ spoke to people who believed, and for the most part believed firmly and extensively, in the supernatural: in a real and living God. We might say from the philosophical point of view that it is not

elementary enough for those who today question the existence of the supernatural altogether. The Christian way of
life, no doubt, can only be gained through knowledge of
Christ; but the logical and epistemological basis of Christian metaphysics, in the first instance at least, requires a
different starting-place.

4

Knowledge of God

In this chapter I want to try to narrow one gap which must be immediately obvious to anyone who has some knowledge both of modern philosophy and of Christianity. One way of observing this gap is to consider the enormous differences in style, technique and apparently also in purpose between any piece of philosophical writing or criticism, like the present work, and (say) the Gospels or the *Imitatio Christi*. Surely, we might think, if we are all anxious to get at the truth of religion, at least one of these methods of approach must be misconceived.

Philosophy, of course, has its own defence. Truth is a matter of language, at least in part: and therefore, to attain truth we must first investigate the conditions for true statements, in particular their meaning and verification. After we have done this (as one professional philosopher told me) 'we have simply to collect the evidence'. All this sounds very plausible. But what is the religious defence? In the Gospels, for instance, we find commands and injunctions ('Follow Me'), statements about the supernatural ('I and the Father are one'), accounts of things done and things suffered (the Crucifixion), and so on. How precisely do these enable us to obtain truth? They do not, after all, read like a typical collection of statements purporting to convey truth: they are not at all similar to a scientific textbook, a

Latin grammar, or a piece of philosophical clarification. Yet it is on them that the Christian truth is supposed to be established. How, then, does what Christ said and did give us increased knowledge?

Philosophers commonly distinguish between three kinds of knowledge, or three uses of 'know'; and this distinction affords a useful starting-point. First, there is 'knowing how' to do something: as when we say, 'He knows how to swim.' Second, there is 'knowing that' something is so: as, 'He knows that the earth goes round the sun.' Third, there is simply 'knowing' by direct acquaintance: as, 'He knows London like the back of his hand.' Between these three types of knowledge there are certain important relations, which must be pointed out:

1. 'Knowing how' is not necessarily connected in logic with either of the other two types of knowing. This is fairly obvious in the case of 'knowing that', but not so plain in the case of knowing by acquaintance. For example, I can know how to swim or how to walk without knowing that the specific gravity of water is high enough to support me, that the muscles in my legs act in such-and-such a way, that I am using two legs, and so on. It is probable that I do know that certain things are so, if I know how to do certain things; but it is not logically necessary. But can I swim without knowing water or some other fluid? or can I walk without knowing or being acquainted with the motions of my legs? In practice, it looks as if 'knowing how' nearly always implied some acquaintance with something. Yet not always: infants know how to breathe, scream, and so on, but it is doubtful whether we could say that they

knew anything by acquaintance, in any full sense of 'know'. We conclude, therefore, that 'knowing how' is not logically dependent on other sorts of knowing.

2. Equally, 'knowing that' something is so is not logically dependent upon the other two sorts of knowing. I may know a great many facts about swimming without knowing how to swim, and I may know a great many facts about London without knowing or having acquaintance with London at all.

3. Less obviously, 'knowing' by acquaintance does not necessarily involve 'knowing that'. I may know London very well indeed, in the sense that I can find my way to and from anywhere without any difficulty, get on the right bus, etc., without having to know a great many facts about London. In such cases, which are not uncommon, we usually say that the person concerned 'does it by instinct', 'sense of direction', and so on. It is not even necessary to know that something exists; though of course when we have acquaintance with something we generally know that it exists. I could be quite well acquainted with what was actually a live human being, but believe throughout that I was talking to a ghost. If someone asked me, 'Do you know that there exists a man named Bloggs, whom I saw you talking to last night?' my appropriate answer would be, 'No, I didn't know that, I thought it was my imagination.' 'Knowing' by acquaintance does not necessarily entail propositional knowledge, knowledge that certain statements are true or that certain things are so. Dogs and other animals know people, but we are not thereby compelled to say that they know that they are people, or that anything else is the case.

4. Notwithstanding the fact that a person can know in any of these three senses without necessarily knowing in any of the others, any statement that he knows, if it is a true statement, does entail other statements. To make this clearer, let us take an example. If the statement 'He knows how to speak German' is true, then it must be true that there is such a thing as speaking and such a language as German: although the man who knows how to speak German need not know these facts also. Secondly, if the statement 'He knows that the earth goes round the sun' is true, then the earth and the sun must exist. Finally, and most important of all for our purposes, if the statement 'He knows Bloggs' is true, then there must be such a thing (or such a person) as Bloggs.

We may now begin to apply some of these points. We asked, 'How does what Christ said and did give us increased knowledge?' To this we might think it appropriate to answer that through Christ 'we come to know God'. But this answer is not by itself wholly convincing, though I believe that it contains the germ of a fuller and more persuasive reply. For if we are to say, and believe, that we know God, then there must be such a being as God. The statement 'we know God', just like 'He knows Bloggs', is not self-guaranteeing: if it is true, and if we are to know it to be true, then we must also know that there is such a being as God. For a rational and logical belief in 'we know God', therefore, a rational and logical belief in 'God exists' is necessary. From a logical point of view, though not necessarily in practice, we arrive at 'we know God' via 'God exists', and not the other way round. We cannot, in other words, logically defend 'God exists' by 'we know God', since in order to defend the latter we have to bring in the former; and this makes our argument circular.

Precisely the same point applies to all similar statements, such as 'we experience God', 'we feel the power of God', and so forth. All these statements in themselves entail asserting the existence of a being (God), and cannot be used to support such assertions. Yet this is plainly not the end of the matter. Suppose I say: 'How do you know that there is such a person as Bloggs?' it would be quite proper for you to reply: 'Why, my dear fellow, because I know him, of course,' if this was true. In this case we do seem to be treating 'I know Bloggs' as a reason for 'Bloggs exists'. And this appears to contradict what we said earlier. Has something gone wrong with the argument?

Nothing has gone wrong with the argument, because the statement 'I know Bloggs', as it appears in this context and example, is used in a slightly peculiar way. Normally the statement would only be made when the existence of Bloggs is not in question. Thus in answer to the question, 'By the way, do you know Bloggs?' we might say, 'Oh yes, I know Bloggs'; or if Bloggs owes me money, I might say, 'He'll repay me all right: I know Bloggs.' But in our example, when we are giving a reason for believing in Bloggs' existence, we are saying something like: 'I have had certain experiences (meeting a man, learning his name on reliable authority, etc.) as a result of which I believe that there is such a person as Bloggs: moreover, I have the honour of being acquainted with him.' Of course this is not intended as a translation of 'I know Bloggs', nor does all this cross our minds when we make the statement. But nevertheless, since the statement functions as a reason, that is its logic and use.

This brings out the chief point about 'we know God' in connection with God's existence: namely, that both the statement 'God exists' and the (logically subsequent) statement 'we know God' must be based on certain experiences: experiences which justify the belief that God exists and that we have acquaintance with Him. In defending the logic of Christian theism, therefore, it is strictly inappropriate to offer 'we know God' as a fundamental basis of belief, since it leaves open the question of His existence. But we could say something like: 'We have certain experiences (in prayer, worship, confession, etc., perhaps) which justify our belief that God exists: moreover, we are directly acquainted with Him.' This is not to say that 'we know God' is an inapposite reply, much less that it is untrue: it is no more inapposite than 'I know Bloggs' in answer to 'Does Bloggs exist?' But plainly, both answers require further explanation and evidence: they are not self-sufficient.

To say that we come to know God through Christ, therefore, is to say that Christ enables us to have certain experiences which form the logical basis for our belief in God: that Christ gives us the ability to know that God exists. But it is not only to say this. Besides the 'knowing that', there is also a 'knowing how' and a 'knowing' by acquaintance. There is such a thing as knowing how to get into touch with God, knowing how to worship, pray, behave, and so on: and there is also such a thing as direct acquaintance with God. Both these, it is claimed by Christians, can be attained through Christ. And though we may admit that truth is a property of statements, and therefore that only 'knowing that' is directly concerned with truth, the two other types of knowing plainly play a very great part in our beliefs.

The part they play is also concerned with our ability to have certain experiences: experiences which are highly relevant to our beliefs, and also — though this is not strictly germane to our subject — of enormous practical significance to the Christian. To take an analogy: suppose I am trying to teach someone to enjoy music. If I am eventually successful, my pupil will be able to exercise all three types of knowledge. He will know *how* to listen to music in general, and to particular pieces of music: he will know *that* Beethoven's Third symphony is heroic, his Sixth beautiful, etc.: and he will know by acquaintance the qualities and characteristics of certain composers and works. Now all these three types of knowledge, in this case, are very much interrelated: it is unlikely that I should succeed in teaching him to exercise one type without teaching him to exercise the others also. Of course this is possible; since, as we have seen, no type logically entails any other type. I might enable someone to have direct experience of various works, or to know how to listen to them, without enabling him to know very many facts; and he would not be very much worse off.

Perhaps now we can see why the fundamental Christian documents, and the Author of Christianity Himself, are not concerned with philosophical analysis or scientific proof. These are no use to the beginner; just as they would be no use to my music pupil. What we need is experience: or, even more basically, we need to learn how to have the experience. Throughout the Gospels, Christ is saying and acting the injunction, 'Try it and see.' That is why His words contain so many commands: 'Follow me,' 'Judge not,' 'Pray in this way,' 'Seek, and ye shall find,' and so on. He teaches us to know *how:* the Lord's Prayer was the answer to the disciples' request, 'Teach us *how* to pray.' He teaches us the direct acquaintance with God: 'He that hath seen Me hath seen the Father.' And as a result of all this teaching, if we choose to establish and cling to a number of statements or doctrines as well as merely having the experiences, He teaches us *that* certain things are so; and this includes the whole corpus of Christian truth. As He said, 'I am the way, the truth, and the life.'

It is the essential interdependence of these three types of knowledge that so many people find to be a stumbling-block to acquiring religious belief. As unbelievers, they are presented with some statement such as 'God so loved the world that He sent His only-begotten Son to save it'. How is he to know *that* this statement is true? How, indeed, is he even to understand the meaning of the words and phrases involved? He can see clearly enough that God is not supposed to have loved the world in the same sense that I loved chocolates as a child, that Christ is not His Son in the same sense that I am my father's son. Consequently he is tempted either to dismiss it as nonsense, or at the least regard it as incomprehensible. Similarly, to repeat an analogy already used, a tone-deaf person with no knowledge of music would find it baffling if a musician were to tell him that a certain composition was 'sad' or 'tragic'. Plainly these words are not used in their normal sense; the musician enjoys listening to the music he calls 'sad': he may weep, but they are not tears of common grief. Yet they mean something.

Yet to talk of music as 'sad' is not to talk vaguely or ambiguously: anyone with a wide experience of music, particularly if they are well acquainted with the compositions under discussion, knows exactly and immediately what is meant. He knows this, because he knows and has had the experiences to which 'sad' refers. He has had, we might say, direct acquaintance with the sadness of music. We might add also, that he has had this acquaintance because he has learnt and knows *how* to listen to music, by dint of long practice and training.

In precisely the same logical way, by following Christ, listening to His words, seeing how He acts, praying to Him and so forth, we come to have experiences of an unambiguous and unique character. We learn to describe these experiences by words like 'God', 'loved', 'the Son of God', etc. Finally we are in a position to make our original statement, 'God so loved the world. . . .' All this, however, represents a long and difficult process. First, there is the knowing *how*: how to pray, how to allow Christ to speak to us, how to worship, how to behave towards our neighbours. Here we are (to put it at its lowest) 'going through the motions': learning by doing what we are told to do, or by trying to do it. This is, indeed, one of the most common ways in which we learn as children, by imitating our parents and other adults, and going through drills and movements prescribed by them. In the second place, we come as a result of this to have certain experiences. Obviously it would be impossible to describe these without using the descriptive words which have been chosen for the purpose

('God', 'love', etc.). We can give them a meaning for the unbeliever, in the sense that we can translate them into different words: for instance, we can translate 'God' into 'the almighty and perfect Being Who presides over the universe'. But plainly we cannot cash the words into the unbeliever's own experience, since he has not had the experience. Similarly we can translate words like 'red' and 'green' into other words, and thus teach a blind man their meaning: but we cannot cash them into experience which he has not had. Finally, we can formulate these experiences in words and statements, which will hold good if they faithfully represent the experiences they are supposed to describe: if they pass the verification-tests. In this way it can be seen that the three types of knowing with which we have been concerned are very closely linked. To attempt to speak sensibly about God without the training and practice which make experience possible is as absurd as to talk about music without appreciating it.

Learning to be Christians is much more like learning to appreciate music for the first time than it is like learning science, because we are all beginners; and also because it is not so easy to obtain the experiences which we seek as it is to obtain experiences of material objects, which are the subject-matter of science. Most of our efforts are correctly spent — correctly, even from the point of view of someone who is interested in assessing Christian truth rather than leading a Christian life — in trying to do those actions and have those thoughts and be those sorts of people which will enable us, as it were, to get inside our subject. For a Christian, this involves prayer, worship, communion, confession, and the rest of Christian discipline, both ritualistic and moral. Only through that discipline can we attain knowledge, because only through that discipline can we attain the experience we need. If we succeed in the discipline and attain the experience, learning both to 'know how' and to know by acquaintance, then there is a sense in which our knowing *that* various Christian statements are true is of secondary importance; just as to a music-lover, rather than a music critic, knowing of facts is less important than enjoying and appreciating the music, and approaching it in the right spirit. The person with true Christian experience knows more about religion, in the most important sense of 'knows', than the most acute philosopher; and that is why — thank goodness — philosophy is not requisite to salvation.

5

Science and Religion

It is no longer fashionable, in philosophical circles, to speak of a 'conflict' between science and religion. Philosophers are apt to say, as they often say of two parties to a dispute, or two views which are apparently mutually exclusive, 'they do different jobs.' The job of science is to predict, describe and explain: the job of religion is — well, that is more difficult, of course. We can say that it is to tell us about God or the supernatural, to create and uphold faith in us, to fill us with moral strength, and so on. Just how these jobs are done by religion is left obscure; but it seems to be agreed that they do not include prediction, description or explanation. That would be to challenge science on its own ground (the claim goes), and we don't want to do that. We have learnt that lesson from the nineteenth-century Genesis dispute, at least. Let each keep to his own sphere of knowledge.

This claim is all very well, provided we know just what the spheres of knowledge occupied by science and religion are. But this is entirely unclear; so unclear, indeed, that many people doubt whether there is such a thing as religious knowledge at all; and even if there is, they are not sure how it works. Even if it is inappropriate to speak of a conflict, therefore, there certainly exists a tension and an anxiety; an anxiety felt by many intelligent Christians

that science may swallow up religion, if not by open conflict, then by stealth. It might appear that this has already
happened to some extent. Christianity seems to be continually yielding ground before the advance of science.
Where will it all end? Perhaps Christians have already lost
the battle by unconsciously yielding to science and the
philosophers all that they need; perhaps there is no knowledge, or no type of knowledge, left to which religion may
justifiably lay claim.

Two examples should make our position plain. First, the
Christian belief in the Creation, as expressed in the statement 'God made the world'. We no longer believe that He
did so in 4004 B.C., perhaps; but many of us believe that
He did so at a definite time. We treat the statement as referring to an event, assuming 'made' to be used, as normally, in the past historic tense. Let us use x for the date on
which God made the world. This entails that at some time,
namely any time before x, the world did not exist: this remains true however remote x may be. Now suppose that
there is no scientific evidence for this entailment; suppose,
even, that there is a good deal of evidence for the belief that
the world has always existed — for the 'continuous creation' theory, for instance. What does the Christian do now?
He may give up his belief in the Creation as an event
having a definite date; he may even give up the belief *in
toto*. If he does so, it becomes clear that his belief falls in the
realm of science, since his acceptance of scientific evidence
shows that it is verified by scientific methods. Alternatively,
he may still retain the belief, whatever the scientific evidence; and this shows, by contrast, that it is not a scientific
belief. If we wish to retain the belief as religiously and not

merely scientifically significant, we shall probably adopt the latter view. But then we feel inclined to ask just what is the significance of the belief: just how it is supposed to be verified: just how we believe it to be true. If the statement, 'God made the world,' represents a piece of religious knowledge, how do we know it is really knowledge, and what sort of knowledge is it?

Our difficulties over miracles are of much the same type. We believe that God divided the Red Sea, that Christ healed lepers, and so on. Now, suppose that scientists (including psychologists) could fully explain and describe these phenomena in terms of scientific knowledge. After all, there is no reason why scientific methods should not be able to do this; science has explained unusual events before now. What does the Christian do? Again, he has two choices. He can either take these explanations seriously, and if he finds that they are as adequate for these events as they are for others, he can give up his belief that the events are miraculous. This suggests that 'miracle' means for him something for which scientific evidence cannot (logically) give an explanation: that in calling some event miraculous he means that it is in principle scientifically unexplainable. Or he can disregard the scientific evidence, thus removing his belief from the realm of science altogether. But the question remains, into what realm has he removed it? We may say, the realm of religion: but this hardly clarifies the matter. What are we asserting when we say, 'God divided the Red Sea,' if this assertion is neither verifiable nor falsifiable by scientific evidence?

There is, of course, a third possible attitude. We may continue to find fault with and question the scientific evidence *ad nauseam*, in the hope of finding a loophole through which we can, as it were, squeeze in the supernatural. We may continue to ask, e.g., 'Can we really be sure that there wasn't a sudden act of creation at some time?' or, 'Is it really proved beyond doubt that something curious didn't happen, when the Red Sea divided, besides all the scientific explanations we've had?' This view reminds one of the various attempts to escape from the imagined 'chain of causality' (supposed to be some form of compulsion) in the physical world by pointing to the unpredictability of electrons and sub-microscopic entities. The attempts are misconceived; and if this sort of view is taken, then the impression that Christianity must retreat as science advances is a correct one. In any case, the view is hardly consistent with a reasonable attitude to evidence and rational belief; since it is rational to believe what is probably true, not only what is certain. It is certainly not rational to believe what is improbable.

Attempts to solve this problem, or to lessen this anxiety, have been many and various. Nearly all the disputes, however, seem to come to grief over a fairly simple ambiguity in the meaning of 'science' and 'scientific'. Probably because we take the physical sciences as a model for 'science' as a whole, there is a prevalent opinion that the realm of science includes the whole of the natural world, 'natural' being defined in terms of what is ultimately verifiable by sense-experience. It is tacitly assumed that all knowledge stems from sense-experience (except knowledge of analytic truths, as in mathematics); and the implied conclusion is that there is no knowledge of the supernatural — if indeed 'supernatural' has any meaning. The reason why it seems sometimes as if science will swallow religion is that most believers still treat their beliefs as if they were scientific beliefs: e.g. 'God made the world' is supposed to refer to an event; but then they feel unwilling about accepting scientific methods of verification until the evidence is overwhelming. And if 'science' refers only to the natural world, the world of the five senses, then of course this unwillingness is very proper. We should feel justified in saying that scientific verification, in this sense, had no connection with religious statements at all.

We might, however, understand 'science' in a wider sense, to refer to sophisticated knowledge of an empirical kind, whether derived from the five senses or not, and whether about the natural world or not. This would probably also involve a shift in the meaning of 'empirical' away from 'derivable from sense-experience' towards 'derivable from any type of experience'. And in this sense, we need have no fear about religion being swallowed by science. Our anxiety would be neurotic; for nothing would prevent religious truth being a part of scientific truth, in the wide sense of 'scientific'. We are, after all, not concerned merely with repelling the word 'science', but in repelling the implication that only the known sciences, or only natural sciences, can give us knowledge. If 'science' is enlarged to include the supernatural, we should be quite content to let 'science' in this sense swallow religion.

And this, of course, shows us where the conflict really lies. The physical sciences have challenged religion rather than conflicted with it. They have challenged it by setting up a standard of verification which religion has lacked; and the anxiety displayed by religious believers is the anxiety of those who are not sure where to look for verification of their beliefs, and therefore fear — not without reasons — that those beliefs are likely to fall under scientific verification, as it were by default. It can only be allayed by the contention (which I have made in a previous essay) that these religious statements are informative, and are ultimately verifiable by a special type of experience, namely religious experience or experience of the supernatural; and together with this contention must go the determination to view the meaning of such statements as 'God made the world' and 'God divided the Red Sea' in the light of this sort of verification.

Certainly, then, religious statements must be regarded as descriptive. We can say they describe the world, provided we remember that 'world' here includes more than the natural world, i.e. the world of physical science. In this enlarged sense of 'scientific', they could be called scientific statements. But 'science' normally implies, if it does not entail, more than simple description or common observation. Science involves more than the notation of everyday facts. It must be in some sense sophisticated: it must be not merely common sense, but 'organised common sense', to quote a common definition. It implies today the existence of special techniques of observation and theory-building. Above all, it implies the ability for prediction and explanation, to a higher degree than would be possible if it did not exist. Its reputation and appeal, indeed, derive chiefly from this ability: it is the scope, cohesion, and predictive accuracy of scientific hypotheses which make us speak of 'the wonders of science'.

Now there is no reason why religion should be able to

compete with these characteristics of science. We should have to admit that knowledge of the supernatural was very difficult to obtain, and that at present we could do little more than observe and describe. Religion may occupy a position similar to that of psychology before the introduction of scientific method and theorising, when what we now call psychology was largely a matter of commonsense observation. We could even go so far as to admit that religion was a sort of backward science, still in its infancy, and perhaps hardly deserving to be categorised under the heading of 'science' (in the normal sense) at all. That should not worry us; the importance of religious truth need not be proportionate to the ease of acquiring it.

The questions of whether religion can do more than merely describe and whether it could (logically) predict and explain in a truly scientific manner, however, remain to be answered. It is generally believed that such prediction and explanation is no part of religion. Hume, followed by most philosophers today, claimed that religious believers had exactly the same expectations about the future as unbelievers, thereby suggesting that their religious knowledge had no predictive or explanatory value. Yet most Christians would surely be unwilling to accept this position. If an event occurs, such as the dividing of the Red Sea, and we make the statement 'God divided the Red Sea,' we should certainly want to say that the fact here referred to (whatever it is) could be used not merely to describe the event, but also in some sense to explain it.

This suggests that we must hold that, in those cases where we want to say that the supernatural influences or interferes with the natural world, as in miracles, a complete explanation of the natural event must involve some reference to supernatural facts or experiences. In accounting for or explaining the occurrence of miracles, this does not seem to me at all unlikely or absurd. Consider, for example, a case of faith-healing. We could give some account, or explanation, of the cure in physical terms, showing (say) how the sudden increase in the power of the sufferer's antibodies, glands, hormones, etc., led to a rapid recovery of health. We could add to this by a psychological explanation of how people in certain states of mind can influence their bodies in this unusual way. But the fact, if it were a fact, that the healer was at the time having certain experiences of a supernatural kind (in Christian terms, was in contact with the power of God) would also be relevant to an explanation. If we knew that certain people, when confronted with sick persons, could seek and find religious experiences that would enable them to cure them, our predictive powers would be enhanced considerably.

This seems to be by far the most promising line for a believer in miracles to take. We must suppose that in every miracle, there is a person involved who through his experience of the supernatural is able to make use of unusual powers. This experience would be a necessary part of the explanation. One might find, for instance, that without taking religious experience into account psychology could not explain these unusual events satisfactorily; and one might be able to demonstrate a verifiable link between this experience (in certain contexts) and an unusual control over the physical world. The miracle would not be supernatural in the (degenerated) sense of contrary to all reason, essentially unpredictable, etc.; but it would be supernatural in the sense of being (partly) caused by experiences of the supernatural or spiritual world.

Note that this does not mean that we can drag in the supernatural whenever we fail to give a satisfactory natural explanation; for the answer may lie merely in more hard work in investigating the natural world. We may be able fully to explain many events, which we now take as miracles, by physical science; and in that case, we must either drop the word 'miracle' or admit that a miracle may have no religious significance. Religious experience must be evidently relevant to these events, not just imported by wishful thinking. And, of course, the physical and psychological scientists are not likely to take the relevance of supernatural experiences seriously, unless we can show that these experiences are genuine and important, and do affect the natural world; unless we can show it at least possible, for instance, that in calling down fire for the altar Elijah was in contact with God, that Moses' faith and prayers were relevant to the dividing of the Red Sea, that Christ's closeness to (or identity with) God accounted for His paranormal powers, and so on. This puts the onus upon religion. It must be able to produce cases where the supernatural must be brought in, by the scientists' own standards of explanation. And it will only be able to do this if it can provide some method of isolating and testing the power and properties of religious experience.

By contrast, the scientists must not revel in the progress and achievements of the physical sciences at the cost of making a simple philosophical mistake: the mistake of thinking that there is some logical reason why all experience, or all cognitive experience, experience which gives rise to knowledge and truth, must be sense-experience. Logical necessity does not enter into it. To say 'there must be a natural explanation' is not to utter a tautology: it is to express a creed. There may, however, come a point at which the creed becomes untenable. The creed of 'there must be an explanation' will survive, however; and surely this is all that scientists need. It is as absurd to cling to the word 'natural' as it is to the word 'supernatural'; and to assume that the one stands for 'explainable' and the other 'unexplainable' is merely silly.

We must be careful, however, about choosing the statements which we regard as explanatory, or as referring to events. Personally I should not care to treat any statements in this way, except those which refer to miracles. Other statements, like 'God made the world', 'God sent His Son', 'God will judge the world for the last time', and so on, run into difficulties which are insuperable. Besides this, such beliefs often involve us in contradictions within the Christian framework. Thus the belief in the Last Judgement, if we take the word 'last' in a straightforward sense, seems to conflict with the belief that God's mercy is everlasting: that a loving God is, so to speak, always prepared to re-try sinners. This difficulty can only be evaded by not treating the Last Judgement as an event. Whether the doctrine will survive this treatment I do not know: certainly many Christians would have to change their minds about it.

For these reasons, therefore, it appears that the 'conflict' between science and religion is indeed unnecessary, but that the anxiety felt about science by religious believers is not wholly absurd. It will only be allayed, however, by providing religious statements with a proper method of verification: a method which will stand up to scientific standards, without involving itself in the physical sciences. For although the conflict may be unnecessary, it does not represent a hoax. It is not true, as so many modern writers suggest, that religious believers have simply been mistaken in supposing that religious statements are intended to be informative and verifiable in the same sense that scientific statements are informative and verifiable. On the contrary, if religion is to survive these are precisely the criteria which religious statements have to (and can) satisfy. If religion gives up this point, then indeed the matter will go by default.

6

Freedom and Evil

The first problem with which we shall deal in this section is one which has disturbed many religious believers for many centuries. It worries alike the lofty theologian and the humble layman; for freedom of choice and the evil that exists in the world both seem to all of us to be undeniable facts. Yet when they are combined with the Christian belief in God's goodness and omnipotence, they present us with a serious problem, whose apparent insolubility has shaken the faith of many Christians, and prevented many other people from ever acquiring that faith.

To say that this is largely a problem of language may sound implausible, but it is true; and perhaps the implausibility may be lessened when we remember that the concepts of freedom and evil, together with the words which represent them, have both given serious trouble to philosophers, quite apart from the difficulties of fitting them into the context of religious belief. Questions like, 'Are we ever really free?' and 'Does evil really exist?' have puzzled many thinkers, from Plato and Augustine to Kant and Hume. When puzzles of this kind arise, puzzles which involve words like 'free' and 'evil' which we use very frequently in our everyday life, the modern philosopher begins to suspect that a thorough examination of these common words is necessary. He suspects that we have got ourselves into difficulties by our failure to appreciate the use and meaning of these words: perhaps just because they are so common, we have never bothered to find out how they work.

In considering the specifically Christian problems of this chapter, we shall not need to go fully into all the linguistic difficulties which trouble philosophers. We shall find, once we have set the problem properly in order, that it turns on two concepts only: on what we are to mean by 'free', and on what we are to mean by 'omnipotent'. It is the clash between these two which precipitates the Christian problem: and we shall see that the clash can only be prevented from turning into an accident fatal to Christian belief by a close consideration of these two ideas.

God is omnipotent and omniscient: God is good: there is evil in the world. We may wrap up the problem of evil in as many complications as we wish, but it consists essentially of discovering whether we can rationally believe all of these statements, and if so in what sense. To consider the statements in a simple form affords us some clue to the answer. For most people would admit, at least *prima facie*, that the first statement is more liable to ambiguity and confusion than the other two; and also, I think, most religious believers would jettison the first rather than the other two if they were logically compelled to jettison one of them. They would hold out strongly in favour of God's goodness, and the existence of evil; but they might under pressure be prepared to modify their belief in God's omnipotence or omniscience.

There have been many attempts to justify this triad of

statements; by the claim, for instance, that the evil in the world is only apparent, and not real. Only two, however, have ever seemed really plausible, or gained very much popularity; and I shall confine myself to a consideration of these two alone. First, there is the claim that the evil in the world does not mean that this world is not the best possible, because evil is necessary if there is to be true goodness and true virtue. Evil is needed that the good may shine more brightly. Secondly, there is the claim that evil, though not strictly necessary for goodness, is an unfortunate and perhaps inevitable by-product of human freedom or free will: and that this freedom is so essential to true goodness that God has correctly chosen to allow it even at the cost of evil. Freedom includes freedom to choose wrongly; and if God wants us to be truly free, He must allow us to choose wrongly whenever we do so.

The first view, I think, has gained credence chiefly from the picture of human life in this world which portrays goodness chiefly or wholly in terms of victory over evil or temptation. Many people admire the man who is by nature not wholly good, but who conquers his wickedness, more than the man who by nature is inclined to virtue. What seems admirable to them is not so much being good as winning moral battles over evil. The man who resists temptation is better than he who never feels it. From this it is but a step to saying that vice and evil must exist if there is to be virtue and goodness. Some people must be poor and hungry if other people are to display charity and generosity towards them; and the existence of pain and danger is necessary for the exercise of physical courage. The world is, and ought to be, a kind of battle-school or training-ground: an assault-course for virtue. For the present state of man, this is the best possible arrangement.

Of course many arguments can be and have been brought against this view. We might point out: (i) that on this view we ought not to go too far in remedying evil, since we should then abolish our assault-course: presumably we should feed the hungry, but not so efficiently as to abolish hunger: struggle against our bad characters, but not so successfully as to leave no evil in us to fight against. If we were all so virtuous, and fought so successfully, that we removed most or all of the evil in the world, then (on this theory) the world would no longer be the best possible. The view seems to entail that we should be virtuous, but not too virtuous, or not too successful in our virtue. This seems a queer conclusion: (ii) that we have no assurance that the assault-course is of the right difficulty, i.e. that it produces the maximum of virtue. It might be too hard or too easy: or too hard for some people and too easy for others. Many people struggle against evil and are over-whelmed by it: many others seem to have no struggle at all. In neither case is virtue triumphant. To assert that this is the best of all possible worlds, despite the evil in it, would entail asserting that the evil in the world was of exactly the right quantity and quality: not too little, not too much, but just right. This would be hard to show: (iii) that we can still display virtue without the actual existence of evil, in resisting temptation: just as the loyal angels in *Paradise Lost*, for instance, displayed loyalty by not seceding from God: (iv) that virtue is only a means to an end, a method or instrument for producing goodness, and that we only admire it because it does produce goodness, or good states of affairs. Thus we can only assess whether a man is virtuous, or how virtuous he is, by seeing whether he does good actions or is likely to do so.

These considerations seem to me — and I suspect to most people, once they have weighed them well — to make the theory implausible. But it would be a logical mistake to regard them as conclusive. For no-one can logically prove or disprove that this is or is not the best of all possible worlds. The issue is not a factual one, and not capable of logical proof or disproof. It depends on one's personal values. The most one can hope to do, as I have just been doing, is to point to considerations which might influence these values. But these considerations are not conclusive. It might be possible to entrap somebody who held this view into being logically inconsistent or inconsistent with known facts. Thus he might say both that the existence of evil is good and necessary, and that it would be better if we abolished it altogether: this is a logical inconsistency. Or he might claim that everybody had a chance to be virtuous in certain ways, whereas a psychologist might be able to show that compulsive forces were exercised on some people's minds which overruled this capacity: and his view would then be inconsistent with this fact. These would be points against the view; but apart from this, we can do nothing except demonstrate what the view entails, and ask people whether they still want to hold it.

Linguistically, we would here be asking people for their criteria of goodness: for what they really meant, or wanted to mean, when they called some state of affairs, or human being, 'good.' As I have already suggested, different people have different criteria. What one man means by 'a good man' is not what another means; and no-one can force his criteria or his meaning upon another. If Christians seriously considered certain beliefs, however, I feel that many of them would not wish to adopt the criteria of goodness suggested by the theory we have just criticised. For there are two things which must surely fix the criteria of goodness for Christian believers. 'Good' must have some reference to what is like God, and to the state of affairs which we may crudely call 'being in Heaven'. These, in Christian belief, are the ultimate facts: God and Heaven exist permanently, and our world is but a short sojourn. It seems somewhat inconsistent with Christianity, therefore, to derive criteria of goodness from this world, and not primarily from God's nature or from the heavenly state. Yet it would be queer to say that we call God, or those in the heavenly state, 'good' primarily because He and they are continually overcoming temptation or rejecting the lure of vice. Indeed, the very notion of God or His saints overcoming some temptations (to adultery, to theft, or to drunkenness, for instance) seems rather absurd. It seems much more reasonable for a Christian, therefore, to fix his meaning of 'good' by reference to what men are, rather than by reference to the moral victories which they win. I think this is a case, one among many, where religious believers have been unduly influenced by the world; and where a careful, philosophical consideration of their own moral thinking, particularly as regards the choice of criteria and meaning for their moral world, would perhaps cause them to change their minds.

I think in fact that few people would still want to hold the view we have been considering, and that nearly all would fall back on the second theory: the free will defence. According to this theory, God has created us free, and cannot interfere with our wrong choices without taking away our freedom. This is obviously correct: if we are not free to do wrong, but are prevented from doing so by God's interference or compulsion, then we are not free. We may also admit, what is essential to the theory, that this freedom is worth all the evil and suffering which it engenders. Even further, we may be prepared to grant that all the evil in the world is due to an abuse of freedom; and where this seems implausible (for instance in reference to disease, earthquakes, etc.) we may even be prepared to postulate the existence of a Devil who has misused his freedom and is responsible for these evils. These admissions give the air of trying to save the theory at all costs, but there is no compulsive reason why they should not be made.

What destroys the theory, however, is that it entails a concept of freedom which is not only unsatisfactory but self-defeating. This point has been made at length by other writers, and needs only a short exposition. Briefly, 'free' does not entail 'uncaused' or 'unpredictable': it entails only 'uncompelled'. The type of moral freedom or free will with which we are concerned when we discuss vice and virtue, evil and goodness, does not necessitate indeterminacy, in the sense of uncaused and unpredictable choices. It necessitates only the absence of compulsion. To demand indeterminacy in this sense is self-defeating, for it would mean that nothing — unless we cared to talk of 'chance' — controlled our choices. If they were not the result of anterior states of mind, character, motives, etc., but entirely without cause or origin and in principle unpredictable, then our choices would be purely haphazard: if indeed we can conceive of such a thing. Yet for moral freedom it is essential that something should control our actions, namely ourselves. When it is the man himself, and not something outside him, which chooses, we say he is free. We may well be able to predict his choice, and know its causes: as for instance if a man with a deep sense of honour repays a debt. The man is still free, because his sense of honour is part of him: he is controlling his choices and actions. Yet it might be possible to trace the psychological origins of his character in general and his sense of honour in particular. We may take God Himself as another example: we can predict that God will always love us, because He is love. We know the cause: it is part of His nature. But this does not imply that God is compelled or not free; for only some causes are compulsions.

It follows, therefore, that it would be possible to have people who were entirely free and yet always chose rightly. These people would have perfect characters, i.e. characters which always resisted temptation. And the theory breaks down just here; for if God is omnipotent, why did He not or does He not arrange that men had characters of this sort? In simple Biblical terms, why did He not make Adam and Eve so that they resisted the serpent's temptation? He could have done so, and still left them free. As we have seen, it is perfectly possible to have people who never do evil and are still free: we do not have to choose between sinners and robots.

If God created or made us, in any straightforward sense of 'create' and 'make', then evidently He made us the sort of people who would choose wrongly and do evil on occasion. Moreover (and here His omniscience comes in) He must have been able to foresee this. Indeed, many reputable Christians have pictured God as foreseeing it: Milton does this in *Paradise Lost*, for instance. And if He could predict it, why did He not do something about it? The only answers seem to be, either that He could not, in which case He is not omnipotent or omniscient, or that He would not, in which case He is not entirely good. For (except on theories like the first of our two views, which seem very implausible) it does not seem to be good to create people who do evil.

This does not entail, as some have thought, that we are not to blame for our wrong choices. Except when we are under compulsion, we are to blame, because we (and not some alien force) have chosen and acted. We acted freely: it is our fault, and we are responsible. But God does not thereby evade responsibility for having created us as we are; and indirectly, therefore, for our evil choices. Similarly we might blame a young man for a wrong action committed freely, and blame his father for not educating him well enough to shun such actions. Or we might say of a badly-made wheel which buckles under strain and thereby wrecks a lorry, 'It was the wheel's fault,' and then go on to say that the wheelwright was to blame, not directly for the accident, but directly for having made a bad wheel and thus indirectly for the accident. The discovery of a cause for someone's action does not exempt him from blame and responsibility, just as it does not exempt him from freedom.

What our analysis does suggest, however, is that the three statements which I mentioned at the beginning,

'God is omnipotent and omniscient', 'God is good', and 'there is evil in the world' cannot be held simultaneously, as long as we interpret them straightforwardly. Attempts to interpret the last two in anything but a straightforward way are bound to end in failure; but the first is more questionable. What makes the statements inconsistent, as we have seen, is the notion of a God Who has created, or Who could have created, perfect human beings (in the sense of their always choosing rightly), but Who plainly has not done so. This difficulty arises whether or not we believe that there was an act of special creation for man (as in the Adam and Eve story). For even if we think that God so planned the world that imperfect men were the end-result (via evolution, for instance), the argument still holds. An omniscient God would have known His planning would result in imperfection, and an omnipotent one would have been able to remedy it accordingly.

It seems, therefore, as if we must modify our ideas of the creation; and, indeed, as I have suggested elsewhere, statements like 'God made the world' have weighty difficulties of their own. To the question, 'Could God have created perfect men?' we must be bold enough to return the answer, 'No'; and not until we are prepared to do this can we really set about re-thinking God's position *vis-à-vis* the material world. We still tend to think of God as a sort of divine watchmaker, Who makes the machine of the universe, adding perhaps a special gadget by creating man, and occasionally interfering with the works by means of miracles, but generally allowing it to run on undisturbed in its perfection. This picture will not do, and leads to the logical contradictions we have been considering.

If we do modify these notions, it should not be too much of a struggle to modify the notion of omnipotence also. At present we regard God as omnipotent in the sense of being able to interfere with or adjust the material world as and how He wishes. To say, by contrast, that God is omnipotent only in the supernatural world is not to utter an empty statement; the only reason why it might seem so is that we insist on assessing God in terms of the natural world, and that therefore supernatural omnipotence might seem to us inadequate. It would mean that God can control and order everything that reaches the level of the supernatural, and by that means can exercise an indirect control over the natural. In terms of a concrete example, God *cannot* (not will not) control a man's body or mind unless the man rises to a sufficiently high level — the supernatural level — to obtain His power: God *can* only heal a sick man by faith, not by direct physical manipulation. In principle, the supernatural can (if we permit it) exercise infinite power over the natural world: and all this power is God's. In that sense, God is omnipotent; but His omnipotence is only potential in the natural world, though it is actual in the supernatural.

According to this view, God is all around us, but (as it were) cannot strike until we give the word. He cannot influence us until we ask Him. This view has a certain ring of orthodoxy about it — Christians frequently say that God cannot help us unless we ask Him — but it is not usually taken seriously. If pressed, most Christians would probably say that God *could* influence us and interfere with the natural world, but that He prefers not to; and they would try to fortify this position by the free-will defence. It is true, of course, that God's inability to interfere with the natural world directly is in one sense a limitation of His powers. But it is a limitation which we have to accept; and if we remember that God is a spirit, and not a sort of Superman, the acceptance may come more easily. What makes it hard is that 'supernatural' still means for us 'like the natural, only better, more powerful, efficient, etc.'. There is a sense in which the supernatural is more powerful than the natural; for the supernatural (God) can comprehend, observe, and when possible control the natural world, whereas the converse is not true. But there is also a sense in which they are different worlds, set apart; just as human intelligence is set apart from animal instinct. There are only two ways in which we can influence animals: either by the use of our bodies which we have in common with the animals, or else by the animals' learning to understand the manifestations of our intelligence. We can either drag the dog to the paper-shop and force a newspaper between its teeth, or wait till it comes to understand our order to fetch the newspaper for itself. God is 'without body, parts or passions': to Him only the second way is open. He must wait until we hear Him.

7

Religious Ethics

The philosophical interest in meaning and verification which we noticed in the first section of this book extends far beyond its immediate relevance to the metaphysical statements of religion. For in regarding statements in the light of their verification, the philosopher has not confined himself to one type of statement alone. He has not been able to do so; for he has found that the meaning, verification and general logical status of statements vary very widely.

One linguistic discovery in particular has had a great impact upon contemporary thought: namely, the discovery of the logical differences between empirical and moral language, between words like 'red', 'square', 'apple' and 'weight' on the one hand, and words like 'good', 'right', 'ought' and 'duty' on the other. These differences can be put in various ways. We may say that the first are used solely to *describe*: to refer, ultimately, to certain experiences of the outside world which we have or could have; whereas the second are used to *value*: to commend, praise, blame, advocate, and in general to set some kind of price upon the outside world which we experience. To use an analogy, descriptive words are rather like the numbers, columns, squares and so on on a roulette board, which we all agree by common experience to be there: value-words resemble the chips which we ourselves choose to place on one square or the other.

This explains the differences, which we have all vaguely noticed in our lives, between arguments about fact and arguments about morality. We are all agreed when to call something 'red': if the majority of people call it so, if it has a certain refractive index in terms of light-waves, and so on, then it *must* be red — 'must', because this is what 'red' actually means. But words like 'good' do not work like this. Primarily, 'good' does not describe experiences at all: it is used to commend certain features of our experience. Thus, two people might agree about the facts — about all the features of their experience: yet one of them might call the situation good, wishing to commend it, and the other might refuse to do so, since he did not wish to commend it. We all have our own standards of goodness, our own criteria for applying the word 'good' to things or people: and though we may happen to agree about many standards and criteria, we are not logically compelled to do so.

The general development of moral philosophy, which stems primarily from these facts of language, must impinge very forcibly on those whose morality is claimed to derive from their religion. It might look at first sight as if morality cannot be logically based on religious belief, since morality cannot logically be based on anything at all. If the truth of morality cannot be proved — if indeed the notions of 'truth' and 'proof' do not apply to morality at all, but only to descriptive language and arguments about facts — then it is no use trying to prove its truth by religion, or by anything else. All this should seriously upset the believer, since one of the advantages of religious belief is supposed to be that it gives one a moral code to guide one's life.

Let us try and see just what it is that the philosophers have done. Certainly they have succeeded in pointing out important logical and epistemological differences between moral thinking and empirical thinking, between valuing and learning or knowing. No amount of facts, no number of empirical characteristics, can logically compel us to accept something as good, right, our duty, or in any way valuable; unless, of course, we already hold the view that anything with these characteristics is valuable. Values, though not matters of taste and therefore not trivial nor arbitrary, are matters of personal preference, choice, decision or attitude. They are not matters of fact.

All this has been shown many times by many philosophers, from Hume onwards; and it would be rash to challenge it, at least in this general form. The importance of such a view for religious ethics is plain. For if it is true, we cannot deduce or otherwise prove that any religious morality is correct simply from a consideration of religious beliefs about the characteristics of the supernatural. Our experiences of (or beliefs about) God, for instance, could not force us into any ethical conclusions about Him or anything else unless they already contained ethical premises. For factual experiences and beliefs do not by themselves warrant ethical conclusions. The often-quoted remarks of Hume, to the effect that one cannot derive an 'ought' from an 'is', hold good.

This point is a purely logical one, and applies whether we are dealing with the natural world or with the supernatural. The facts of psychology and the facts of religion are equally powerless to impose values upon us. We do not escape the point just because we choose to base our morality on the mystical and supernatural, rather than on (say) the crude hedonism of the early utilitarians, who are perhaps more usual objects of philosophical attack. What we have to do, if we are to retain our religious ethics, is to show how the point can be accepted without causing any real damage. And this involves showing how morality can be based on religion in a real and encouraging sense, without necessarily being a logically compulsory product of beliefs about the supernatural. We can say, of course, that morality is based on religion psychologically, in the sense that people of a religious disposition, who believe certain religious truths, find it psychologically congenial or helpful to adopt certain moral codes also. But this is obviously not sufficient. We need to show that the basis is rational; and the difficulty is to show this without also trying to show that it is logically compulsive, which it is not and cannot be.

The apparent setback which has happened to religious ethics, however, is largely of our own making. We have had a long history of Protestant-Christian ethics, of which Kant's work is typical, which endeavours to regard moral rules and imperatives as in some way logically compulsive. As a result we tend to regard moral values as objectively real and existing in the same sort of way as objects or properties exist. 'Duty', 'morality', 'virtue' and so on pose before us as concrete entities. Very often this results in some sort of intuitionist view, whereby one can 'see' what is valuable by intuition, much as one sees what is yellow by eyesight. Consequently we have not been very concerned to discover reasons for our ethical beliefs: we suppose that such reasons

G

are unnecessary. When philosophers show us, therefore, that there is no logical basis for this type of ethical theory, we are somewhat at a loss. We may (as several philosophers have done) fight a kind of secondary action, and point out that this sort of theory is at least useful in showing how we actually do our moral thinking and use moral words; but what we cannot do is to give satisfactory and fundamental reasons why people should adopt our morality.

What precisely could count as a satisfactory reason for a moral belief, however, is not very clear. Once we decide to adhere to a moral standard, rule or criterion, of course, then factual evidence can count as a good reason. If I decide not to cause other people unhappiness, then to point out that in stealing Smith's umbrella I would be causing Smith unhappiness would be to give me a good reason for not stealing Smith's umbrella. But what reason could be given to me for making my original decision? I might decide that I did not care about other people's un-happiness at all. Presumably, I could be shown that this would probably involve my being punished by the law. But I might not care about being punished. I could be shown that this punishment would make me unhappy. But I might not care about being unhappy. And so on.

In considering a typical case of this kind, however, it generally becomes obvious that the person who resists all the suggestions which are offered to him as 'good reasons' must be rather queer; though this does not mean that he can be logically compelled if he chooses to resist. The reason why he seems queer is that he appears to be indifferent, not only about other people's lives and happiness — this is common enough — but about his own. This makes one suspect that he may not want to be rational in making his moral decisions at all: that he has no end or objective in life in terms of which alone good reasons could be presented to him. In other words, there seems some reason to believe that if enough facts of the right sort are brought forward, they would be found psychologically though not logically compelling to a rational person.

This sounds quite plausible where people have to make decisions which affect only or chiefly their own lives. We could produce good reasons for not becoming a drunkard, an opium addict, etc.: reasons which would boil down to saying, 'Don't do this, because it won't really give you the sort of life which you want: you'll regret it afterwards, find it psychologically unsatisfactory, etc.' If our hearer still decides to thwart his own ends, and thinks that it is right for him to become a drunkard or an addict, then he is acting irrationally. If one does not wish to act rationally, of course, there is no sense in asking for good reasons. In these cases, then, there is reason to hope that as our knowledge of relevant facts — particularly psychological and sociological facts — increases, so we shall be able to offer better reasons for individual actions and choices. Some support is given to this theory by the fact that we tend to disagree more in those cases where the relevant facts are not forthcoming. Thus, most rational people accept the common morality about stealing, becoming an addict, driving dangerously, etc., because we know the results of possible choices in these fields; whereas with sexual morality, for instance, we are not sure what types of choices have what effects, and thus have much more room for disagreement.

But the view is less convincing when applied to what are

surely more typical moral situations: namely, those where the end or objective of one person or group appears to conflict with that of another. If, for instance, my objective is power and wealth, this is virtually certain to conflict with other people who have a similar objective. Even here it is possible to say that an objective of this kind would not be found really satisfying; that it is not what a rationally-minded person (after due considerations of psychological facts) would really want. But it is much less plausible. Many people would simply say, 'I'm sorry, but after considering all the facts I still want power and wealth; are there any good reasons why I shouldn't make my choices and decisions with this end in view?' And since we cannot show that the psychological facts *ought* to be relevant to his objective, we cannot show that he ought to accept our 'good reasons': for they are not good reasons to him, but only to those who decide to reject power and wealth as objectives.

It is here, I believe, that religious ethics have a far stronger case than naturalistic ethics, and should in principle be able to produce rational conviction and agreement on moral issues far more effectively. For most religions claim to be in possession of facts which far more people — perhaps everybody — would accept as relevant, indeed decisive, to their choice of objectives: facts about the after life, about God's judgement on sinners, about the long-term effects of certain choices and decisions on the immortal personality of man. Here again, the tendency to regard commonly-accepted morality as something obvious to all men, which does not need to be bolstered up by threats or bribes, is perhaps unfortunate. For it has obscured the essential logic of religious ethics, which is the same as the logic of any other sort of reasonable ethics: namely, the relevance of certain facts to human choices.

It needs only a superficial glance at most religious documents to see how very differently they read from works of morality. In the Bible, for example, and particularly in the teaching of Christ, ethical principles are propounded in two ways. They are not propounded as being logically necessary, or obvious standards which any decently-educated person can 'see'. There is little talk of an abstract 'duty', of virtue for virtue's sake, or of what is 'moral' or 'immoral'. Instead we see (i) straightforward commands and imperatives ('Thou shalt love thy neighbour', 'Judge not', 'Render good for evil', etc.), and (ii) equally straightforward statements of fact, informing us that certain consequences attend upon people who behave in a certain way ('He that sayeth to his brother "Raca" ... is in danger of hell fire', 'He that having set his hand to the plough looketh back, is not fit for the Kingdom of Heaven', etc.). The amount of moralising in most religious documents which is not conducted by these two methods is very small; and this fact should have merited closer attention.

These methods are essentially rational and constructive, because they both depend on the knowledge of facts which are relevant to the objectives of all men. The second method employs this knowledge openly: and the first method is effective if we have reason to believe (as religious believers claim that they have reason to believe) that the person who issues the command, in virtue of his close contact with the supernatural, is doing so because of his expert knowledge in this same field. Often the two methods are used in conjunction, as in 'Judge not' (command) 'that ye be not judged: for with whatsoever measure ye mete, it shall be measured to you again' (relevant fact). The method is essentially like saying, for instance, 'Don't take to opium; for if you do, you'll find yourself unable to do your job, have personal relationships, be contented, etc.'

That the facts which religion claims to be able to bring forward are essentially relevant to everybody, should be obvious to anyone at all acquainted with religion, and I see no reason whatsoever why they should not be brought forward more obviously. The fact (if it is a fact) that to adopt unchristian standards of morality in this life is likely to result in severe discomfort in the next, is very important, and hardly a matter for concealment. To point this out is no more a threat than to point out the consequences of addiction is a threat. It is essential, of course, for religion to be sure of the facts it brings forward: for if they are not facts at all, then the method of persuasion is irrational and unfair, and will in the end be detected as such. But where religion is sure, there should be no hesitation.

Moreover, the facts of the Christian religion at least are extremely encouraging when we are faced with a conflict of ends. To take up but one point, if it is true (as Christ claims) that everyone's most satisfactory life is a life of love — that this is what everyone would really want after due consideration, and that nobody will ever be really happy or contented until he achieves this objective — then a great part of the conflict disappears. For love involves seeking to satisfy the ends of others, and adjusting your own standards of conduct and your own subsidiary objectives to fit in with theirs. Conflict is here logically impossible. In other words, if psychologically compelling reasons can be given for avoiding conflicts with the ends of others, on the ground that such conflicts can only do harm to one's own ends, then conflict becomes irrational.

This is a very welcome conclusion, of course; though it is not a conclusion which has (in practice at least) won general acceptance. The point which the philosophers have made about the logic of ethics has this to teach religion: that we should concentrate essentially upon facts which are relevant, and which we may hope are psychologically compelling, to people as they actually are, having the ends which they actually have. Reasons for moral behaviour are not inaccessible: but neither are they obvious.

8

Immortality[1]

The problem of immortality, or the survival of death, has been the concern of many modern philosophers and theologians. The philosophers, of course, have been concerned, not directly with whether the belief is true, but with its logic, meaning and verification. For what makes this a philosophical problem, and not just a question of fact, is that it is far from clear what the notion of personal survival logically entails. In other words, we are not sure how words like 'I', 'we', 'ourselves', 'survive death', 'same person' and so on really work, both as used in everyday language and in the language of religious belief.

Let us see whether we can point the problem a little more sharply. Many philosophers maintain that the words which we use to refer to human beings — 'I', 'you', 'we', 'man', 'person' and so on — present no particular logical difficulties. They are used, like other nouns and pronouns, to refer to certain complex entities, the entities which we call people. What are people made of? Well, we can list a great many things which go to make up a person — a

[1] The first part of this essay owes a great deal to recent papers on the topic: particularly to Professor Flew's 'Can a Man Witness His Own Funeral?' (*The Hibbert Journal*, April 1956), the Rev. Professor Ramsey's 'What Do Person Words Mean?' (*The Hibbert Journal*, July 1956) and A. C. MacIntyre's 'A Note on Immortality' (*Mind*, July 1955).

body, a brain, desires, memories, spiritual aspirations, and so on. We cannot, of course, list all the components and facets of a man, since there are always new discoveries to be made; but this is not surprising, for we go on learning more and more about physical objects as well as people. We can still know fairly well, however, what we mean by 'a man' or 'a person'. All that we know, of course, about people — all that we mean or could mean by 'a person' — must be based on some form of experience which we have of people: if it were not, we should have no means of distinguishing fact from pure invention. This applies even where we should not want to say that a person was 'made up' of different 'things' or 'composed' of 'different' parts: memories and desires, for instance, are not things in the sense that hands and feet are things. Yet we should not want to talk about memories and desires in relation to the human personality at all, unless we had had some experience of them.

Briefly, the contention based on this is that we do not have experience of any part or facet of the human personality which does or could survive death. Let us say that when we use personal pronouns, or nouns like 'man' or 'person', we are referring to characteristics $a, b, c, d, \ldots n$. Then it is empirically true that none of $a, b, c, d, \ldots n$ survive physical dissolution. At death the heart stops, the pulse ceases, the brain no longer emits its characteristic rhythms, the nerves fail to transmit their impulses: speech, thought, imagination, desire, and spiritual aspiration alike are discontinued. It is, of course, true that the process of decay and dissolution do not always occur at the immediate moment of death, as they might if (for instance) one stood near an exploding atomic bomb. But apart from this trivial truth, all the evidence goes to show that every characteristic from *a* to *n* vanishes without hope of recovery.

The most common attempt to escape from this attack, and one of the most ancient, is to postulate two or more fundamentally different parts or facets of the human personality: summarily, we may call these the body and the soul. According to this defence, the body admittedly dies and decays: but the soul lives on. The soul has always been conceived of as something at best only half-physical and rarefied, more usually non-material altogether. Thus in Homer the 'shades' are literally shadows of their former selves: in Plato, on the other hand, the soul appears as something intangible and immaterial, as it does in Christian theology. Almost it seems that this concept of the soul was (consciously or unconsciously) devised so that it should be the sort of thing which (perhaps by definition) escaped physical death and decay.

So far as personal immortality is concerned, particularly in Christian belief, this theory will not do, for several reasons.

1. It appears to be based on a false and naïve concept of a human being, whereby a man is regarded as divisible into separate parts, some 'material' and others 'immaterial'. But as soon as we begin to speak of the human personality in non-material language, we have to drop the notion of 'parts', at least as a serious concept. 'Memories', 'desires', 'love' and so on are not words which refer to parts of people, except in a very loose sense of 'parts'. They are

phenomena, but they are not disconnected phenomena. We have evidence that they are affected by our physical state; and we have no evidence that there is a 'part' of the human personality which is not so affected, remaining immune to the extent of being able to flit away immediately our physical personality dissolves.

2. The theory does not save a belief in personal immortality, unless it can show that *we* survive death. To say that our souls survive death is not necessarily to say that we do. In other words, the theory has to show that 'soul' includes enough of the characteristics *a, b, c, d, . . . n* for us to say that the person originally composed of these characteristics still exists after death. Here we begin to ask questions like, 'What are the essential criteria of personal identity?' If a man loses his body, his memory, his desires, etc., is he still the same man: or more precisely, does 'he' refer to the same person both before and after the change? How much can we give up, and still remain ourselves? These are interesting questions, but it does not look as if the answers will be very hopeful for the present theory. For most of what we mean by 'he', 'man', etc., (if not all) cannot reasonably be allotted to the 'soul part' of man. *a, b, c, d, . . . n* are for the most part characteristics like bodies, memories, desires and so on which, by all the evidence, do cease at death. If a man were to lose all these, he would cease to be a man: or at least, he would cease to be the same man.

3. The theory is not (in my view) consistent with the best Christian doctrines of immortality, nor — what is perhaps more significant to some people — with what each of us actually hopes for when we hope for immortality. How-

ever the doctrine of the Resurrection of the body be interpreted, and whatever meaning may be given to the Christian hope, it certainly includes more than the continued
existence of an immaterial soul. Our memories, our characters, and our bodies all have a place in both the Christian
and the common belief. All these parts or facets of our
personalities may (whatever this might mean) be trans-
formed into a different sphere, become spiritualised, etc.,
but they must at all costs remain ours: otherwise we are
not surviving in the sense we require. The theory seems to
condemn us to saying that we survive only in the sense in
which we might say 'the spirit of Nelson lives on', which
seems to be largely if not entirely metaphorical.

A second type of defence consists of a sophisticated and
improved version of the first type. It does not speak of the
soul as a part of the human personality, in this hitherto
rather crude sense; but it claims that some of the characteristics $a, b, c, d, \ldots n$ are such that they would survive
death. This defence is a natural development from the
first. Moreover, it is a defence which is very much on the
defensive, if I may so put it. Its supporters say to the philosopher, in effect: 'Can we really be sure that all the observed characteristics of personality, $a, b, c, d, \ldots n$, are all
the characteristics there are? Is it not possible that "I",
"we", and "a person" are not more than these? We do not
believe in anything so crude as a *thing* or *part* called a soul,
of course; but there might be some aspect of the personality
which you have omitted. At least you cannot prove that all
our characteristics disappear at death.'

The danger with this defence is that it may become so

rarefied as to approach vacuity. Professor Ramsey, for instance, writes:[1] 'Is personal behaviour no more than behaviour which is observable or in principle observable . . . ?' It is not clear whether he thinks the answer to this should be yes or no; and plainly neither answer will really do. If we say yes, we commit ourselves to saying that aspects of our personalities are in principle unobservable; and in this case, it is in principle impossible that we should ever use them as evidence of personal immortality. For if we could not in principle observe them or have some experience of them, how do we know what they are like? Or how do we know that they exist? Or (worse) would it mean anything to say that they did exist? On the other hand, if we say no, then it is doubtful whether we can prove that any observable characteristics are likely to survive death.

The defence is open to the last two objections which applied to the first defence, though it avoids the first objection. Although (1) we no longer have to talk about the soul as a part of man, we still have to show (2) that these immortal characteristics or aspects are ourselves, and (3) that they include all those necessary to sustain the Christian belief in the Resurrection. As a result of the rarefaction of this defence, difficulties (2) and (3) become much more severe. For it is more plausible to say that we are our souls, and therefore we will have life after death in the Christian sense, than to try and identify ourselves with certain obscure aspects or facets of our personalities even more tenuous than the soul, and then to claim that these are sufficient for Christian belief. By abandoning the crudity of the soul we have also abandoned its substance:

[1] Op. cit., p. 331.

a substance necessary to uphold the Resurrection. Thus, when Ramsey says that our awareness of our personalities 'covers all . . . public behaviour, *and more*' (his italics), we may perhaps agree. But it is not at all clear that this 'more' is anything like enough. For we wish that we ourselves should survive: and this certainly includes a great deal that could come under the heading of 'public behaviour', in the sense of publicly verifiable behaviour. For our desires, memories, character and so on, besides our body, are publicly verifiable in a perfectly good sense.

The doctrine of the Resurrection, including the Resurrection of the body, is surely not to be defended in this way at all. For we have to say (1) that our present bodies decay and disappear after death, and yet (2) that we have bodies after death. How are we to verify the second statement? Ultimately we must do so, as with all other religious assertions, by reference to religious experience. We could say, then, that the immortality of our characteristics (which will now include all or most of $a, b, c, d, \ldots n$) is in principle observable: though this does not mean that we have to say that it is observable by just anyone — any more than God is publicly and commonly observable. What we have to do, in order to content the philosopher who does not happen to have the experiences which alone can enable him to verify this, is to show roughly how it could be true.

We should naturally start by denying that words like 'we', 'person', and so forth *must* refer to things which are commonly observed or observed by any normal person. There is nothing queer about this at all, for people can use words as they wish, and plainly do often use them in such a way as to be (in one sense) incomprehensible to those who do not share their experiences. Thus when a music-lover talks about 'that symphony', calling it 'poignant', 'dramatic', and so on, he is not referring merely to something which is commonly and easily verifiable by anyone with the use of his five senses. Similarly religious people claim to have experiences in virtue of which 'person' means something more, or something different, from what a non-believer might mean by it.

Next we should point out that to say that all the parts or aspects of a thing have disappeared or been destroyed is not to say that the thing itself has disappeared or ceased to exist. We may remember the old problem about the axe. Its owner says: 'I've had this axe for twenty years: in that time it's had three new heads and four new handles.' All its parts have gone, and been replaced: but it is still the same axe. And to say it is still the same axe is not to utter mere metaphor or idiom. On this analogy it is plainly logically possible to say: 'Jones has existed now for hundreds of years: he lost his body, brain cells, etc., last December, but he's still the same man.'

What this suggests, surely, is that religious believers may think of a person primarily in terms of a *pattern*, not as simply a collection of characteristics. When $a, b, c, d, \ldots n$ disappear, we may admit that they do genuinely disappear: provided we insist that these are only natural characteristics. Yet they are *replaceable*; and the way in which they are replaced does not destroy the pattern of personal identity. For every natural characteristic (a) there is (in principle) a supernatural characteristic (A). We may believe, then, that men consist, or could under certain conditions consist, of both these types of characteristics: our list would then look like $a(A)$, $b(B)$, $c(C)$, $d(D)$, ... $n(N)$. When a, b, c, d, ... n disappear, A, B, C, D, ... N take their places. Moreover A, B, C, D, ... N are *like* a, b, c, d, ... n. At death we are changed — this is admitted by all parties: but we are not changed beyond recognition.

One point is important here. The words of Christ, and other Christian authorities, do not or should not lead us to suppose that immortality is inescapable, or will be the same for all people. 'He that believeth in Me, shall never die' does not necessarily imply that he that believeth not shall never die either: quite the reverse. One might believe, even, that immortality is something to be won: that our achieving immortality depends at least partly upon how much we cultivate our supernatural characteristics, and how much we are content to remain on the natural level. A man in whom A, B, C, D, ... N are very real and important characteristics might be thought more likely to survive, or to survive with less radical changes, than a man for whom a, b, c, d, ... n were more important. We do not know whether we have the power wholly to extinguish our supernatural characteristics; but we have at least an inkling that the degree to which we attend to them and realise them in the natural world is significant for our survival as people.

Perhaps an example will make this clear. It could not be an exact parallel, of course; because we are here dealing with two different levels of experience and order (natural and supernatural), of which the supernatural is only observable to some people: whereas any example from the natural world will involve reference to what is publicly observable throughout. Suppose we know nothing about the roots of a tree: 'tree' means for us only what is apparent above the level of the ground. Then, if a tree suddenly snaps off, so that nothing above the ground is visible, and is chopped up into firewood, we would say that the tree had ceased to exist. But in fact this would not be so. If the tree had strong roots, and had not foolishly expended all its energies on flowers and foliage, it would still exist: and it would be able to replace its lost trunk and branches. Moreover, these replaced parts would be similar to the ones it had lost: it would still be the same tree.

What Christians claim is that man's supernatural characteristics, like the roots of trees in this example, are immortal: and that under certain conditions at least they are capable of reproducing or replacing (whether immediately after death or not) the natural characteristics which have disappeared. Under these circumstances one might well say, as Christians do, that the man has not really died, but changed: perhaps for the better, just as a rose-bush pruned level with the ground may produce a better growth. And though this belief may be hard to prove in practice, there does not now seem to be any logical or philosophical reason why it should be absurd or peculiar.

9

The Doctrine of the Trinity

We turn now to a particularly difficult problem, which depends for a full solution not only upon clear thinking but also upon a scholarly interpretation, and a wide knowledge, of the historical contents of a great many Christian statements. I hope to show, however, that even here the approach via a study of the language and logic involved is a necessary one. We saw in the first section of this book how useful was the tool of verification which modern philosophers have placed in our hands: and in the last chapter, when we dealt with personal immortality, we observed the importance of the problem of personal identity, which for its solution relied on a close analysis of words like 'person', and the personal pronouns ('I', 'he', and so on) which stand for persons. Here too we shall be concerned with the analysis of the important words 'person', 'nature', 'substance' and certain other phrases, round which the whole problem of the Trinity turns.

I have spoken of 'the problem': but in fact there is a whole family of problems which are generated by Trinitarian doctrine. One of the initial difficulties is to discover just what 'Trinitarian doctrine' stands for: to discover precisely what our subject-matter consists of. A question like, 'What is the doctrine of the Trinity?' is impossible to answer if one does not know the sectarian context in which it is asked: different churches have different doctrines. The question, 'What is a common (perhaps the most common) doctrine of the Trinity?' however, is much easier. It is for no sectarian reason, therefore, that I choose some statements of the Thirty-Nine Articles as representative of common Trinitarian doctrine. The statements could be found in a slightly modified or expanded form in many other places — the *Quicunque Vult*, for instance. My reason for using them as a basis of discussion is simply that they are brief, lucid, and in general unexceptionable to nearly all Trinitarians.

In Article I we read: 'There is but one living and true God . . . without body, parts or passions. . . . And in unity of this Godhead there be three persons of one substance, power and eternity: the Father, the Son, and the Holy Ghost.' In Article II: 'The Son, which is the Word of the Father . . . the very and eternal God, of one substance with the Father, took man's nature . . . so that two whole and perfect natures, that is to say the Godhead and Manhood, were joined together in one person, never to be divided, whereof is one Christ, very God and very man. . . .'

Christian apologists point out indefatigably and correctly that these doctrines arose as an attempt to formulate the experiences of early Christians in language. They are — indeed to be informative they must be — based on experience; and we are not here concerned to question the genuineness of that experience, or to try and detract from it. But if religious language and doctrine are worth anything at all, it is important that the statements should be both comprehensible and free from logical contradiction

and difficulty. And of course the Church has always recognised this: the Councils of Nicaea, Constantinople and
Chalcedon did not convene purposelessly. Yet the difficulties remain; and with the development of modern logic
and epistemology it becomes even more necessary to over-
come them.

Trying to make religious doctrines of this (technical)
kind square with modern epistemology is an enormous
task; though it is a task which will have to be undertaken,
if religion is to answer the criticisms which arise from it,
and which will continue to arise until answered. We shall
here concern ourselves with two central problems. First,
we need to examine the meaning and use of the Trinity-
in-Unity concept, as exemplified in Article I; and second,
we need to analyse the very-God-and-very-man concept,
as exemplified in Article II.

The first thing one notices is that the philosophical terminology of the Articles is now outdated. This is not to say
anything so silly as that it is 'wrong', or vitiates their truth:
terminologies are not (like statements) wrong or right, but
(like tools) more or less useful. The technical terms about
which we feel in some doubt nowadays are (i) 'substance'
('*essentia*' in Article I: yet 'of one substance' in Article II is
'*consubstantialis*') (ii) 'person' ('*persona*' throughout), and
(iii) 'nature' ('*natura*' throughout). The uses and abuses of
the concept of substance are well known to philosophers:
the concepts of 'person' and 'nature' also are liable to con-
siderable fluctuations and ambiguities. Part of our problem
will be to provide a suitable interpretation of the doctrine
which avoids the use of these technical and doubtful terms.

1. 'There is but one . . . God.' This seems fairly straight-

forward. Only one entity which satisfies all the criteria for our descriptive word 'God' exists. This seems to be like saying, 'There is only one Winston Churchill.' The monotheistic point is added to by saying that God is 'without parts': in modern English this would be 'indivisible' ('*impartibilis*'). Yet we are told that 'in unity of this Godhead there be three persons'; and this appears to conflict, if not with the first part of this point, at least with the second.

A popular solution consists in interpreting 'person' in such a way that a person in this sense is not an entity. We could say, to take a common suggestion, that 'person' here means 'rôle': a suggestion supported by the Latin 'persona', which means something more like 'rôle' than 'individual'. For it looks as if to accept 'person' in the modern sense of 'individual' will not do; we should then have to say that there were three individuals (three persons) in one individual (one God), and this looks dangerously like a logical contradiction. Yet this attempt has its own difficulties. We feel hesitant about saying that God the Father, Christ, and the Holy Ghost — but particularly Christ — are not persons in a fuller sense than the one suggested. Christ is surely not just a rôle: He is a real person. On the other hand, if the three persons of the Trinity are entities, then God is not one entity but three. Hence our dilemma.

Let us consider analogies along these lines more fully, however. We may say: 'There is only one Winston Churchill. Yet he is Prime Minister, Defence Minister, and the Leader of the Conservative Party.' Now apply our questions to this analogy. Can Churchill be divided? In the sense that he can play different rôles (hold down different

jobs), yes: but not in any other sense. He cannot be divided
as Churchill: but it might be sense of a kind to say that he
can be divided as a politician — he can play three political
parts. To take another analogy: a wicket can be divided
into its three stumps and two bails. Yet there might be only
one wicket. It cannot be divided and remain a wicket, in
the way that a piece of wood can be divided and remain
a piece of wood. We can say, if we like to put it like this,
that 'wicket' is used to refer to a complex entity.

Next question: are Churchill's rôles persons in the
modern sense? Plainly one *can* answer 'yes' to this question.
This would be the natural answer to the question: 'Is the
Prime Minister a person?' or 'Is the Defence Minister a
person?' The fact that the Prime Minister and the Defence
Minister are persons does not make Churchill into a sort of
super-person or super-entity. Similarly, the fact that a
wicket is a thing does not mean that stumps and bails are
not things; neither does the existence of stumps and bails as
things make the wicket a super-thing.

Another question we could ask might be: what is the
relation of the rôles or persons to Churchill? Supposing we
ask, 'Whom did you meet yesterday?' and are answered,
'The Prime Minister.' We go on: 'Are you sure it wasn't
Winston Churchill?' Answer: 'Yes, of course it was, you
know who the Prime Minister is.' This suggests that 'Prime
Minister', 'Defence Minister' and 'Leader of the Conservative Party' are just three descriptions of the same
person. Indeed they are three descriptions of the same person: but they are not *just* that. It would be inappropriate,
if one was asked, 'Who is today responsible for leading the
Conservative Party?' to reply, 'The Defence Minister.' A

title is not merely an alternative description. It calls attention to a rôle or a part played by its owner. Thus it would
be incorrect to say that 'the Defence Minister is Winston
Churchill' *identifies* the Defence Minister with Winston
Churchill. Nor must 'Winston Churchill' here be an adjec-
tival phrase (as one might suspect, for instance, with 'and
the Word was God', coming as it does after 'the Word was
with God').

Of course 'part' may be ambiguous. It might mean
'rôle', as with Churchill: but it might be interpreted at
least on an analogy with physical objects. The stumps are
all parts of a wicket. Consider the Churchill dialogue as
applied to this case. Question: 'What did your ball hit?'
Answer: 'The middle stump.' Question: 'Are you sure it
wasn't the wicket?' Answer: 'Yes, of course it was, you
know the middle stump's part of the wicket.' Yet in this
case it is plain that 'middle stump' and 'wicket' are not
alternative descriptions, nor anything like them. Again,
the statement (which we can imagine made by an irate
umpire, for instance, under suitable circumstances) 'the
middle stump *is* the wicket, you ass', does not identify the
middle stump with the wicket, nor does it use 'the wicket'
adjectivally.

The apparent contradictions of the Trinity-in-Unity concept derive from the temptation to ask questions like, 'Are
there *really* three persons, or only one?' The deceptiveness
of such questions is brought out more strongly by the
wicket analogy than by the Churchill one. For in the case
of Churchill we feel inclined to say that there is 'really'
only one person: admittedly, we say, the Defence Minister
is a person, the Prime Minister a person, and the Conser-

vative Leader a person — but 'really' they are all the same person. But suppose we ask of a wicket: 'Are there really three things there, or only one?' What sort of answer could we give, except to say simply that there were three stumps, but only one wicket? Or we could say, perhaps, that it depends on your point of view. If you are a wood-worm seeking bits of wood, then there are three things you are interested in: if you are a batsman, there is only one — though of course the batsman's interest in his wicket does not disqualify him from interest in the three stumps: indeed the one entails the other.

It is not at all absurd to say, therefore, that there are three parts or persons of God, all of which are entities in their own right, but that 'God' is still the name of a single entity. Nor — and this is important — does this remove God into an entirely different and incomprehensible order of existence. There is only one order of existence; things either exist or they do not. Wickets exist, and stumps exist: both are equally real. They exist in the same sense, and the existence of one does not detract from the existence of the other. God cannot be divided and remain God, any more than a wicket can be divided and remain a wicket.

Yet one can see that there is a sense in which God can be regarded as more mysterious or difficult to comprehend than any of His persons. To continue the analogy, we are from the Christian point of view more like wood-worms than batsmen. We find it easier to appreciate an individual stump (Christ) than the total effect of three stumps, joined together to make one wicket. The surface of the earth is not a good place from which to appreciate the importance of wickets. We must climb higher; we must turn into batsmen.

It is now plain that 'substance' can be interpreted quite simply. To say that the three stumps of the wicket are all 'of one substance' will mean simply that they all form part of one entity. To say that the Defence Minister, the Prime Minister and the Conservative Leader are all 'of one substance' will mean that they are all parts (in another sense) of Churchill. One would expect, what one actually finds, that both these sorts of parts would have enough characteristics in common with their wholes to describe any of them as 'of one substance' with those wholes. Thus both stumps and wickets are hard, breakable, made of wood, must not be trodden on by batsmen, etc.: both the Defence Minister and Churchill are powerful, wise, eloquent, and so on. It seems quite possible, therefore, to retain both the logic and the wording of the Articles in this respect: even though we might find 'substance' somewhat obscure.

2. '. . . . took man's nature . . . so that two whole and perfect natures, that is to say, the Godhead and the Manhood, were joined together in one person, never to be divided, whereof is one Christ. . . .' First an important comment on the text. The Latin version (and it is arguable that this represents the opinion of the compilers as well as or better than the English) reads: '. . . ita ut duae naturae, divina et humana, *integre atque perfecte* in unitate personae fuerint inseparabiliter coniunctae. . . .' This should be strictly translated: '. . . so that the two natures, the divine and the human, were inseparably joined together *wholly and completely* in the unity of a person. . . .' In other words, the natures are not qualified in the Latin as being themselves 'whole and perfect': it is the manner of their conjoining that is so qualified.

This is worth pointing out, because of the importance of 'nature'. It is possible (I believe it is correct) to maintain that Christ had two 'natures': but it would be more difficult to maintain that He had two 'whole and perfect natures'. For if we were to ask, 'What is the whole and perfect nature of God?' we should be inclined to give an answer in terms of Article I, saying that God was 'without body, parts or passions', 'consisting of three persons', and so on. The *whole* nature of God would have to include reference to these criteria, and anyone having the whole nature of God would have to satisfy all of them. He would have to *be* God in the sense of being identical with God. We cannot defend the statement 'Christ is God' in that sense: 'Christ' and 'God' are not simply two alternative descriptions (see (1) above). But it is arguable that Christ should be God, not in the sense of identity, but in the sense that the Defence Minister is Churchill, or that stumps are the wicket.

I interpret 'having the nature of' as 'having the essential characteristics of', therefore; and 'having the whole nature of' would thus mean 'having all the characteristics of'. The second is indefensible. Whether the first is defensible depends, of course, on what characteristics are regarded as essential. And here the Christian points to characteristics such as goodness, love, power, etc., rather than to being without parts, having three persons, and so on. So one might consider the essential characteristics of a wicket in terms of its being hard, wooden, important for batsmen, an objective for bowlers, and so on, rather than being made up of three stumps. This singling out of certain characteristics rather than others is not unfair: the question of fairness does not arise. This is simply what the doctrine is.

The same points apply to Christ's human nature. As used by Christians, 'having the nature of man' and 'having the nature of God' are not mutually exclusive. But this does not entail that 'man' and 'God' are alternative descriptions. The essential characteristics of a man, in the way that Christians interpret 'essential characteristics', do not clash with the essential characteristics of God. An example may help here. There is such a thing as being a Jew, and such a thing as being a Fascist. It may be extremely unlikely that a Jew should ever actually be a Fascist; indeed there may be only one person who is both. But he can really be both: there need not necessarily be a pretence. For the essential characteristics, the criteria we use to describe 'a Jew' and 'a Fascist', do not conflict. He might be completely ('perfectly') a Jew, and completely a Fascist: 'very Jew and very Fascist.'

'Person', in the sense of the Articles, need mean only 'a living and intelligent entity'; and there is now no contradiction or difficulty involved in saying that Christ is one person, a part of (consubstantial with) God, and having the essential characteristics of both God and man (having the nature of both God and man). Just as a stump is both a piece of wood and also part of a wicket, and yet is one entity, so Christ is both man and God, and yet one person. Yet here too we meet with something that, though not logically peculiar, is nevertheless mysterious. For Christ is a person in a fuller sense than that in which the Defence Minister is a person: He is a person in the sense in which Winston Churchill is a person. As an entity, it might seem more reasonable to class Him as a wicket rather than as a stump. There is a sense, therefore, in which it is reasonable to say that the entity Who is God, having three persons, is beyond our comprehension. An entity Whose parts are persons is not met with in our experience in the natural world: that is why the Churchill analogy is only an analogy, and useful only to show that the logic of the Trinity is not contradictory or meaningless. The mystery, however, remains; but it is no longer a logical mystery.

10

Sacraments

In many respects the logical problems concerned with the Christian doctrine of the Sacraments represent a classic case where the philosopher can be helpful. For the problems are, above all, concerned with what precisely it is which Christians assert about the Sacraments, and with what method of verification is supposed to be used in supporting these assertions. We shall see that there are, in fact, at least three different verification-methods which we may use: each of which I shall briefly describe, in order that it may be quite clear where our choice lies.

A sacrament, in the sense in which a layman might be interested in the word, is simply a sacred symbol. But the Christian doctrine — or perhaps one should say, Christian doctrines — about the Sacraments is more complicated, and varies considerably from church to church and sect to sect. Even those who hold the broadest of broad church views, however, make some sort of important distinction between sacraments and the Sacraments. Thus Bicknell writes in an authoritative edition and commentary on the Thirty-Nine Articles: 'In the widest sense sacraments are as wide as the world. A blade of grass may be a sacrament. On the other hand, the Church of England . . . uses the word sacrament in a narrower and in a wider sense. In the Catechism it declared that Christ ordained two sacraments only "as generally" (i.e. universally) "necessary to salvation".' The logical problem with which we are here concerned is to see how this distinction can be upheld, for it is a distinction which nearly all Christians make and regard as important. So important is it held to be, indeed, that 'practising Christian' has come to mean almost the same thing as 'communicant', the Holy Communion being regarded as the prime or essential Sacrament.

Now it is plain that there could be many possible reasons for regarding the Sacraments as so important that Christians are prepared to describe them as 'necessary to salvation'. But one can distinguish two general lines of argument or belief in Christian apologetics. They are not mutually exclusive, but may be held separately or in conjunction.

1. It may be held, as the Roman Church seems to hold, that the physical constituents or ritual of the Sacraments has some special power, force or effect of its own: that they are effective in their own right. It is very difficult to state this view clearly without being (perhaps justly) accused of over-simplification. But it is plain, at least, that the quality or property in question does not depend entirely upon the mental and spiritual attitude of those taking part in the Sacrament. Watching the sun rise or listening to Beethoven are not Sacraments: and the reason given, on this view, is not simply that these actions are not based upon religious authority and tradition. It is rather that the true Sacraments — the bread and wine, or the baptismal water — are enjoined by the Church *because* they have a special efficacy of their own. The bread and wine, for instance, actually *are* the body and blood of Christ: they are not

merely symbols which happen to be effective because people are what they are. They are effective because of what they are themselves. Even if we agreed, on some sort of philosophical theory or other, that sunrises and Beethoven were 'objectively' moving to all people under all conditions, this would still not make them Sacraments. Their 'powers' would not be sufficient.

The difficulty with this view, of course, is that the statements which express it are usually unverifiable. By all the standard tests, the bread and wine are ordinary bread and wine. The fact that many people regard them as symbols, and hence are able to gain comfort, grace, strength, etc., by using these symbols, does not mean that they have some kind of magical force. In a very real sense, the view insists on making itself unverifiable: for no verification in terms of feeling-states, added piety, moral improvement, and so on, is permitted. For it is felt that this somehow removes the essential property from the Sacrament, and hands it over to mere mortals. Moreover, if this verification were adopted, it would always be possible that some other sacrament (sunrise or Beethoven) would be found to have better effects; and this result would be intolerable.

I do not propose to discuss this view further, since there is no point in discussing unverifiable statements. This does not mean that they must be nonsense; but neither does it mean that it is a satisfactory defence of the Sacraments to say that they have this special power, and when challenged philosophically to fall back on the position that the whole thing is a Mystery. This position, however, often proves to be a slightly grandiose way of introducing the second type of defence, which is usually held in conjunction with the first.

2. It may be held that we should regard the Sacraments as of special importance on authority. Usually this is either the authority of Christ as recorded in the Bible, or the authority of the Church (early or contemporary). It is generally believed in the Church of England and many other churches, for instance, that Christ 'commanded' or 'instituted' at least two Sacraments — Baptism and the Last Supper; and it is certainly often quoted, in support of the Christian insistence on Sacraments, that the long tradition of the Church in using the Sacraments is of great weight and importance.

I have mentioned elsewhere the difficulties which attach to believing on authority: they apply to this case as to others. But we meet here with some peculiar difficulties of our own, in reference to the two authorities on which we are supposed to rely.

(a) If by saying that Christ 'instituted' the Sacraments it is meant that Christ performed certain actions similar to those that we today perform as Sacraments, and that Christians after Him continued to perform those actions, then it is (probably) true that Christ instituted the Sacraments. But this sense of 'instituted' is in itself insufficient to demonstrate that we have His authority for insisting on their continuance today. The evidence that He intended them to be continued in the conditions of the twentieth century, and in all parts and peoples of the earth, is at the very least not conclusive. On the other hand, if it is meant that Christ ordained them, and definitely enjoined their continuance under all conditions, then it is doubtful whether we possess enough historical evidence for this belief. It is not within the scope of this book to include historical investigation, nor am I at all qualified to do so. But from the point of view of simple logic, it is necessary to remind ourselves that if we are to feel at all certain about Christ's intentions or statements, we must demand evidence of as decisive and unambiguous a kind as we should demand in similar historical contexts: as we should demand, for instance, for feeling certain about the intentions of other historically remote figures, such as Pericles in ancient Athens, or Pompey in ancient Rome. Professional historians of these and similar periods are notoriously suspicious of their evidence. It may be unjust to suppose that New Testament critics have been biased by their religious opinions: but at least it is important to remember that these opinions have no logical relevance to this process of purely historical verification.

All this, of course, may be disputed. But it is worth while observing that the greater the importance of the Sacraments is held to be — and particularly if they are held to be 'necessary' — then the better must be the evidence that Christ actually enjoined all those that came after Him, whatever their psychology, race, or era, to use them. And I do not myself believe that any sort of objective examination of the evidence would persuade one that this was so.

It is perhaps just worth noticing a variant of this argument: namely, the view that we ought to copy Christ's actions in general, and therefore His actions in being baptised and celebrating the Last Supper in particular. There are, of course, many cases in which we think that we should copy His actions: but they are all cases in which we have reason to believe that the same conditions apply to us as to Him. Thus, we ought all of us to help the poor, to love our friends, to sacrifice our lives if necessary, to think of God as our Father, and so on. We do not do these things only because Christ did them: we do them because Christ showed us their value. For there are many things which Christ did which we should not regard as suitable objects of imitation. He was circumcised, worked as a carpenter, rode on a donkey, retired into a garden, and so on. We have no reason to believe that these are essential actions for us. We have to produce additional reasons, therefore, why we should think that the Baptism and the Last Supper (both based on local Jewish customs, though used by Christ to make His own points) fall into the first class rather than into the second. And though it might be possible to think of such reasons, it is doubtful whether they would be compelling to the extent required.

(b) That the Church practised the Sacraments is not in doubt. What is here open to question is whether we are to regard the tradition of the early Church, and the following of that tradition (in highly modified forms) by the later Church, as a compelling reason for insisting on Sacraments today, and claiming that they have the special importance which we assign to them. Again, we meet with the difficulties of accepting even so important an authority as the tradition of the Church as valid for all peoples and all ages. Nor, in fact, is it at all clear that the Church has always regarded the Sacraments in the same light as those who rely on this defence wish to regard them in. These points make the defence far too weak for anyone who is fully alive to the difficulties of rational belief on authority.

What defence, then, are we left with? It seems to me plain, from a consideration of the way in which Christian apologists defend the Sacraments, that we have here an anxiety lest we should be forced to say that whether or not we use the Sacraments is a matter of taste. This concern for established tradition is natural, but unnecessary. For just because we do not think these two defences are strong enough, we are not thereby committed to saying that no defence is strong enough. This remark is obvious enough: but it is nevertheless this sort of reactionary and anxious feeling which lies behind the attempt to make the two defences look stronger than they really are. To permit and encourage, for instance, a situation in which Christians regard it as certain that Christ actually ordained and enjoined the Sacraments upon everyone, in the Gospel story, is to lay oneself open to the charge of intellectual dishonesty: whether or not such a charge is justified.

The chief reason why our anxiety is not allayed is that we feel tempted, in the case of the Sacraments and other symbols, to make a false dichotomy. Briefly, the dichotomy is: Either the Sacraments have some special property of their own (possessing supernatural power, as in (1), or being ordained by Christ and the Church, as in (2)), or else they are 'mere symbols'. The second alternative is regarded as intolerable: therefore the first must somehow be true. It is felt that, if the Sacraments do not have a special property of their own, then we have no reason to insist on their use: we might just as well use any other symbol. It becomes a matter of taste, and can therefore no longer act as a bond uniting Christians of all ages and countries.

But consider an analogy. 'Either English banknotes have some special property of their own (possessing intrinsic value of their own, like goods, or being ordained by authority, as a drug might be prescribed by a doctor), or else they are "mere pieces of paper".' Here the dichotomy is plainly false. Banknotes do not have a special property of their own, but we do have reason to insist on their use: it is not true that we could reasonably permit anyone to use any symbol he liked. The difference between genuine and counterfeit notes is not a matter of taste: and banknotes do indeed represent the unity that exists amongst the English people with regard to monetary matters.

Of course the analogy is not exact at all points. Banknotes are 'necessary' because we have in some sense agreed to use them. They are arbitrary symbols: another symbol would do as well if we all agreed to use it, and provided it was equally convenient to handle. But I think that, although this is a genuine point that can be made in favour of the Sacraments, and one which adds far more weight to the importance of Christian tradition and unity, we can put up a stronger defence still. We want to say that the symbols of the Sacraments are not 'mere' symbols, if this is taken to imply that one symbol is as good as another. We want to say that the symbols of the Sacraments are the best possible symbols to use: and not only that, but that they are so superior to other symbols that we feel entitled to insist upon their use.

Whether or not we say that 'the Sacramental symbols are the best possible symbols to use' is simply one version of saying that they have a special property of their own, is largely a verbal matter, and not basically important. I think myself that it is less misleading to hold that, in assessing the merits of symbols in certain contexts, we are not assessing properties of the symbols: for goodness and merit are not properties, at least in the same sense that redness and yellowness or having magic power are properties. We should assess the merits of symbols, not in the abstract — this would be impossible — but in relation to their effects upon human beings.

This means that the question of whether the Sacramental symbols are superlatively effective must be, at least in part, a psychological one; and surely psychological investigation is the natural and proper way to assess the effectiveness of symbols. In this assessment, of course, the fact (if it is a fact) that generation after generation of Christians has found the Sacramental symbols incalculably beneficial will count as strong evidence. Many Christians will be found to say, moreover, that they were beneficial even when they did not appear to be so. This suggests, what psychologists know already, that the visible and apparent effects of symbols on the conscious mind and behaviour of men are not the only criteria for assessing their efficacy. There is, perhaps, something in the nature and form of the symbols themselves, and the ritual connected with them, that finds fellowship with something deeply buried in the unconscious mind. In this connection one begins to think about dream symbols, universal archetypes, and so on; and to suspect that the Christian conviction of the power of the Sacraments is founded upon psychological facts, even though these facts may not yet be clear.

It is not, however, within the scope of the philosophy of language and logic to determine the truth of any suggestions of this sort. I have made them merely to demonstrate the importance of fixing our methods of verification in reference to our religious beliefs. The Christian belief in the

Sacraments has appeared vulnerable, just because it has relied on wrong methods of verification. We have seen (i) that the defence suggesting that the Sacraments have magical properties is no defence at all, because it removes the possibility of any kind of verification: (ii) that if we fix our verification-method wholly by reference to Christ's direct authority, we shall have to face squarely up to the historical uncertainty of this authority: and this might make the belief more vulnerable and doubtful than most Christians would wish: (iii) that once we properly grasp what is meant by the concept of 'a symbol', we can at once notice that there exists a satisfactory verification-method by which to assess the potency or efficacy of symbols: namely, by observing their psychological effects. Here again, our consideration of language and verification demands that we change our style of thinking radically: but a change of this kind can alone extricate Christian doctrine from an otherwise impossible position.

11

Sin and Judgement

The concept of sin has always been one of the chief planks in the religious platform of Christianity and of most other religions. Yet it is by no means clear precisely what 'sin' is supposed to mean: and some kind of linguistic analysis is all the more necessary when we are confronted with semi-technical phrases like 'original sin', or 'the judgement of God'.

In Chapter 6, when we dealt with the problems presented by freedom, evil and omnipotence, we noticed that many religious problems had already excited the attention of philosophers in a secular context. A consideration of the concept of sin leads inevitably to a consideration of other concepts, and the criteria for the application of words like 'free', 'judge', 'punishment' and so on. For the Christian, many of these words derive their meaning primarily from a network of doctrines about God to which he gives assent: for the lay philosophers, perhaps, their meaning and use must be analysed primarily in terms of common usage. But as I hope already to have made clear throughout this book, this does not imply that there is an unbridgeable gulf fixed between the two. However much support the believer derives from other doctrines, each particular belief must be meaningful and verifiable; and the philosopher, whilst recognising that religion is entitled to its technical terms just as much as science, can do a great deal to elucidate the concepts and words which the believer uses.

The Christian conception of sin is not an easy one to grasp, and I do not pretend to be able to expound it fully and accurately. There are, however, certain philosophical points which any conception of sin would have to meet; and it is with the way in which they can be met that we shall be chiefly concerned. Roughly, Christians believe (*a*) that men sin and are sinful (these may not amount to the same thing), and (*b*) that God judges us and in some sense punishes us for our sins and sinfulness. The chief difficulty is to see how these beliefs can be made to fit in with modern concepts of freedom and the human personality, in such a way that the resultant pattern does not do violence to our other moral views and beliefs about God.

Christians could (and probably do) believe in sin in at least two senses. One of these senses is essentially connected with free will or free choices, whereas the other is not.

1. If a man believes in original sin, what does he believe? He may perhaps believe only that all men, in fact and practice, do evil, act against the will of God, and freely choose what is wrong rather than what is right. But the fact that this seems to omit all meaning in the word 'original' suggests that this is rather a watered-down interpretation. Something more than this must be intended. Is it, then, that all men have a dispositional tendency to do evil (act against the will of God, etc.)? Or, if we prefer a more concrete interpretation, that wickedness is ingrained in the nature of man from birth onwards? Some reference

to heredity, or some permanent characteristic of the human race, seems to be intended by the word 'original': it is presumably this that prompts utterances such as Bicknell's 'we are born into a condition of life in which our full union with God is broken'.[1]

Could we blame people for having this disposition or inherited characteristic? The answer to this is not perhaps so obvious as it might seem. For we might say, e.g., 'He is a drunkard, and I blame him for it.' Drunkenness is a vice or fault. Yet being a drunkard is having a tendency to get drunk. We can legitimately blame not only single action or choices, but also dispositions: a vice is precisely a disposition to do evil. Original sin, like many other dispositions, may form an intrinsic part of a man's character: and surely a man can legitimately be blamed for his character. For a man *is* (in part) his character: character is not merely something which happens to be attached to a person.

On the other hand, blame does somehow seem to be inappropriate here. We may disapprove or condemn, perhaps: but surely one cannot *blame* somebody for something for which he is not and has not been responsible, even if the something forms part of his character. Thus, it is possible to turn a person into a drug addict by force, and his addiction will thereafter become part of his character. Yet, though we might disapprove of and condemn this *situation*, we would hardly blame the *man*. For he could not have helped it: he was not responsible.

If original sin is regarded, therefore, as something inherited or acquired 'through no fault of one's own', then as the phrase itself shows, we can hardly account it a man's

---

[1] E. J. Bicknell, *A Theological Introduction to the Thirty-Nine Articles*, p. 234.

fault if he is subject to it. We could, perhaps, using another sense of 'fault', say that it is a fault *in* him: but we could not say that it is *his fault*. And certainly — this will be important later — we could not reasonably say that he should be 'judged', 'sentenced' or pronounced 'guilty' on the basis of this defect: since these words are essentially tied up with the concept of freedom and responsibility. We should, therefore, regard original sin (on this interpretation) more as a sort of spiritual ill-health, the result of the 'corruption of the nature of every man' from birth.

2. 'Sin', on the other hand, and particularly phrases like 'a mortal sin', 'seven deadly sins', and so on, suggests that we often use the word to refer to particular actions and states of mind. Whilst some of these actions and states of mind might be universally described as 'not our own fault', i.e. forced upon us, there is no doubt that others are free actions and states of mind, for which we ourselves are responsible. This to some extent corresponds to the distinction between 'formal' and 'material' sin in Christian theology, or again to the idea of 'subjective' and 'objective' sin. Provided the general distinction is recognised, however, the terminology is comparatively unimportant.

It is perhaps worth noticing that any attempt to lay down a categorical list of sins is liable to run into logical trouble, if it is supposed (*a*) that one must be morally guilty to be sinful, and (*b*) that certain types of actions always and without exception count as sins. For it is logically impossible, in certain cases, to avoid committing sins in the sense of performing certain actions: yet in these cases, how can one be morally guilty, since one is not morally responsible?

For instance, suppose I am driving (on an errand of mercy) very quickly down a narrow road flanked on one side by a solid stone wall. Suddenly a group of children run out from the other side of the road. Assuming that I know beyond doubt that I must either crash the car into the wall and kill myself and my wife, or continue and kill some of the children, what ought I to do? Murder (if this be murder) is a sin: and suicide (if this be suicide) is another. Yet I cannot avoid committing one of these. This impasse arises, of course, only if we brand all actions of a certain type, without exception and without consideration of responsibility or circumstances, as sins. We may draw the general conclusion that no universal or unexceptionable rules of this kind should be made, if we wish to count moral responsibility as an essential criterion for sinfulness.

In this sense, then, a sin is a wrong action or an evil state of mind which arises through our own responsibility. In other words, we must be acting freely to act sinfully: and the connection between sin and 'free will' has always been close — so close, indeed, that sin is often spoken of as something which can be predicated of the will alone. But it is just here that the difficulties arise. They are, in brief: (i) are we in fact ever really free? and (ii) can we ever know when we are free and when we are not? The importance of these questions is plain. For in order for God or anyone else to judge somebody to have committed a sin, it must be in principle ascertainable (i) that men do sometimes act freely, and (ii) that this particular man was doing so on this particular occasion.

(i) The answer to this question is not very difficult. As

we saw earlier,[1] the fact (if it is a fact) that we can point to causes for all our actions in no way implies that all our actions are compelled. The logical criterion for free action is simply whether it is *we* who act, or something 'outside' ourselves which acts on us, or compels us to perform the action. This distinction between free and compelled action, in terms of 'inside' or 'outside' causes, originates with Aristotle;[2] and its comparative neglect by later ages accounts for much of the fruitless discussion in terms of 'free will' and 'determinism'. Much of this discussion proceeded on the false assumption that causes were compulsions — as if all causes were like the imposition of one man's will upon another man. Some people are still worried by the possibility that psychology might be able to explain, predict, or discover causes for all our actions. Even if this possibility were actualised, however, the worry would still be neurotic. For (to put it crudely) some causes will still count as 'inside' causes, or part of ourselves: so that when we act from these causes, it is we ourselves who are acting. And this means that we are acting freely.

(ii) Can we ever know when we are free and when we are not? This question is more difficult. At present we tend to assume that all our actions are free, except those where we have good reason to suppose that some kind of compulsion is operating. Thus, in a court of law the onus is on the defence to prove that the prisoner did not act of his own free will. The defence may be able to prove various sorts of compulsions. The prisoner may have been physi-

---

[1] See 'Freedom and Evil', Chapter 6; also A. J. Ayer 'Freedom and Necessity', in his *Philosophical Essays*.
[2] *Nichomachean Ethics*, Bk. III, i.

cally forced, threatened with violence; or he may be the victim of psychological compulsion, such as kleptomania or some form of insanity. If any of these can be proved, then the prisoner would not be accounted morally guilty (even though the legal verdict might be 'guilty but insane'). The logic of this moral judgement is evident: for in cases of this sort we do not want to say that the man himself did the action freely, but that something 'outside' him forced him into it. We say, for instance, 'It wasn't his fault: it was his kleptomania that made him steal', or, 'He wasn't responsible for his actions.' And we cannot — logically cannot — punish a man, or account him guilty, for something which he did not do: something for which we lay the responsibility on a compulsive cause 'outside' of him.

Suppose, however, that we just do not know the full explanation (all the causes) of his action. In that case, we could not of course prove that a compulsion operated. But this does not mean that no compulsion did operate. In other words, if we do not know the causes of an action, we are unlikely to be able to classify them as 'inside' or 'outside' causes. Consequently, we are unlikely to be able to say for certain whether the action was freely performed or not. For example, suppose a man suddenly gets up and opens all the windows, leans out, and shouts 'Hi de hi!' in a loud voice. Is this a free action or not? We would assume that it was; but if we subsequently discovered that the action was the (generally inescapable) result of a command given to the man under hypnosis a few hours earlier, we would change our minds, and say that the man was compelled to do it. For now we know the cause for the action;

whereas before we knew about the hypnotic command, we just assumed that the man did it of his own free will. Now, there are compulsive forces of many kinds: and not all of them are so obvious or so easily discovered as hypnotic commands. We have probably no inkling of a great many such forces. The assumption that all our actions are free unless we happen to be acquainted with a compulsion, therefore, seems a naïve one. We must admit, then, that where we are not reasonably certain of the cause, we cannot be certain whether or not the action was free.

Unfortunately this is likely to happen only too often, since our knowledge of psychology (and hence of psychological explanation and causation) is still very sketchy, and likely to remain so for some time to come. But the position is even worse than this. For even when we do know the cause, or can explain, or predict a man's behaviour, on what criterion do we classify that behaviour as arising from 'inside' or 'outside' forces? It is important to realise that this is not a matter of fact. For suppose we can say with certainty that the psychological factors responsible for an action were xyz. Then we ask: 'Does xyz count as "inside" or "outside"?' or 'Is xyz to be regarded as part of the man himself, or as something which operates on the man?' If the first, then we can say that the man himself acted: if the second, that he was acted upon. But the answers to these questions depends solely upon how we wish to use words like 'man', 'person', 'he', etc. We may use them as we wish, either to include or to exclude xyz: this is a matter of choice. Whether an action is to be regarded as free or compulsive, therefore, seems to depend on our decision: on how we choose to regard it. And whilst our choices may be wise or unwise, they cannot be right or wrong in a factual sense.

Perhaps an example may make this clear. Imagine a man who steals something being prosecuted in a court of law. The defence produces psychologists who are able to give a complete case-history of this man. Assume that they can show beyond all reasonable doubt that, though the man is not what we would generally call insane, certain factors (*xyz*) operated in his environment and background: factors which always result in theft when the opportunity arises. They would be able to give a complete explanation of the causes of the man's action. No doubt he could have avoided stealing if things had not been what they were: particularly if *xyz* had not operated. But in fact things were what they were, and *xyz* did operate. It is important to note that *xyz* may include all sorts of factors: his heredity, environment, character, choices, opportunities and so forth. Assume further that the prosecution does not contest this psychological evidence, and that the judge also accepts it. The judge can now take one of two lines (if the law permits him this freedom). Either he can say: 'The fact that this man's action can be fully explained, could have been predicted, and arose from causes entirely understood, makes no difference to his guilt: for these factors, *xyz*, are an intrinsic part of the man. He is a wicked man, and has done a wicked thing: he has a vice in him for which *xyz* are responsible, doubtless. But it is still a vice. He acted freely, because *xyz* is part of him: *he* acted. I do not count *xyz* as an "outside" cause or compulsion.' Or he can say: 'I propose to distinguish between this man and his admittedly criminal tendencies. I shall count these tendencies, for which *xyz* are responsible, as a sort of disease from which the man himself is unfortunately suffering. Consequently, the man himself is not guilty: he is not responsible, but *xyz* are responsible.'

Now there is here no factual issue at stake between the prosecution and defence: nor is the judge in doubt about the facts. He can take either of the two courses mentioned. In practice, there is generally some agreement about which course is appropriate: for instance, if *xyz* represents kleptomania or some form of insanity, we distinguish between the man and *xyz*; whereas if *xyz* represent (say) a tendency to lose one's temper, or to act from motives of jealousy or greed, we do not dissociate the man from *xyz*. On the other hand, disagreements do arise, in courts of law and other places: and as psychology advances they become more frequent. It is not so long ago, after all, that we came to accept certain factors as compulsions: factors like kleptomania. Before this acceptance, kleptomaniacs were punished. Now we regret this. Yet it would still be logically possible to count kleptomania as part of a person, and therefore to say that the person was guilty: only for some reason[1] we do not wish to do this.

We must conclude, therefore, that we cannot know *as a matter of fact only* when we act freely and when we act under compulsion. For, firstly, we do not always know the facts; and secondly, even when we do know the facts, it is a

[1] The reason is, surely, that it has been shown beyond reasonable doubt that punishing kleptomaniacs serves no useful purpose. But a firm believer in the self-sufficient value of retribution is not logically compelled to accept this reason, since he is not interested in useful purposes. However, the fact that few people would punish kleptomaniacs suggests that far fewer people really believe in retribution than is generally supposed.

matter of choice whether we interpret them as cases of free action or as cases of compulsive action. It all depends on our point of view: on how many things, and what sort of things, we choose to include within the circle of what we mean by 'a person', or what we refer to by pronouns like 'he', 'they', 'we', and so on.

All this suggests that the connection of sin with freedom is not a factual one, and therefore not as close as we might have supposed. Considering now the Christian belief that God judges our sins, we can see that our conception of judgement must also be modified. For what happens when God judges us? Presumably He is able to see all the causes for our actions, and can predict them afar off. Does He know when we are free and when we are not? If this question is interpreted as a factual one, the answer is no: for it is logically impossible to know *merely* by a study of facts whether somebody is free or not. A more helpful question to ask, then, is, 'What point of view does God take?' Does He choose to include certain characteristics within the circle of personality, and to exclude others? And does he punish us for the included ones, and absolve us from the excluded? If we take words like 'judge', 'guilt', and 'punishment' seriously, we must presumably believe that God does make hard and fast distinctions of this kind, much as a human judge does. But on what basis does he make them, and what is His purpose in so doing?

This introduces the question of the purpose which lies behind judgement and punishment, and behind the assessment of people as 'guilty' (free) or 'not guilty' (compelled or forced). And here, of course, different people hold different views. Some people believe in retribution as a good thing in itself: an ultimate moral principle which ought to be fulfilled, quite apart from its deterrent or reformatory effects. Others do not. I do not propose to try and argue anybody out of a belief in retribution as an end in itself, since ultimate moral principles are not conclusively arguable in this fashion. But there are certain logical consequences for Christian belief which must be faced.

The importance of these consequences may best be shown thus. 'Punishment' means the infliction of something unpleasant and painful on somebody who has done a wrong action voluntarily, *for* his wrongdoing. You cannot, in strict parlance, be punished for nothing: it is more correct to say in such cases that you are being victimised. This shows that the notion of requital or retribution lies at the root of what we mean by 'punishment'. It is essentially a requital of evil by some form of unpleasantness: if a man who had done wrong voluntarily were treated in a pleasant way, we could not call it punishment. The essential feature of 'judging', 'condemning' or 'finding guilty' is also concerned with voluntary wrongdoing. A judge finds out whether a man has done wrong voluntarily: if he has, he can be condemned and found guilty, and then punished. Hence, if you are interested in judging, condemning, finding guilty, and punishing, you must also be interested in whether the action was voluntary or involuntary. If it was voluntary and wrong, then you can punish the man by doing something unpleasant to him.

'Retributive punishment', therefore, is basically a tautological phrase: part of the meaning of 'punishment' is that it should be retributive. This presents us with a choice of attitudes which is far more fundamental than we thought.

It is no longer just a question of whether we believe in 'retributive punishment' or not: it is a question of whether we believe in punishment or not; and not only punishment, but all the cognate concepts of 'judging' and 'condemning' that go with it. If we think retribution a good thing in itself, quite apart from its results, then we must opt for punishment, judging, condemning, etc. If we do not, we have no need to involve ourselves with these concepts. We could talk only about 'treatment' or 'deterrents'. On this second view instruments which are now instruments of judgement and punishment, like the law courts, would simply become institutions whose function it would be to assess the best treatment for criminals, having regard both to the protection of society and the interests of the criminal.

Two logical difficulties stand in the way of accepting punishment and its cognate concepts as morally desirable.

(i) To accept retribution as an ultimate moral principle, as morally desirable in itself, means that we cannot give reasons for defending it in terms of other principles or ends. We cannot say, e.g., that retribution is good because it deters criminals or reforms them: for that would not be to claim retribution as an ultimate principle or end, but as a subordinate principle or a means to an end. We must simply believe that the infliction of pain or unpleasantness in certain cases (i.e. on evildoers) is a good thing in itself. Stated as it now is in this rather more transparent form, I am not sure whether many people would hold to this belief. But those who persist in it can only do so at the cost of a certain inconsistency. If it is held, as most Christians surely hold, that the infliction of pain or unpleasantness on others is wrong unless there is some further end or purpose which justifies it, then this is not consistent with a belief in retribution as good in itself: since retribution precisely consists in the infliction of pain or unpleasantness without ulterior justification. Of course it is logically possible to hold that the infliction of pain is generally wrong if there is no ulterior purpose, but not wrong in the case of voluntary evildoers. This view cannot be disproved — proof and disproof are not applicable to ultimate moral criteria: but it looks queer, and I think that Christians should give it more careful consideration.

(ii) If we wish to punish people justly, we have to be sure that they acted freely: since to punish someone for something which was not his fault cannot (logically) be described as just. But in view of what we have observed about freedom, how can we be sure about this? For it is not a factual question, or not merely a factual question: it is a question of what viewpoint we choose to adopt. How do believers in retribution decide when to adopt a viewpoint which will enable them to say that a man acts freely, and when to adopt a viewpoint which will result in saying that he acts under compulsion? Those who believe merely in reformatory and deterrent treatment have some method of deciding: they could say, for instance, that we should adopt whichever viewpoint will produce the best results for the criminal and for society. But this method of assessment is not open to those who believe in retribution as an end in itself. In other words, the answer to 'Ought we to treat this man unpleasantly (punish him)?' depends on the answer to 'did he act freely?', which in turn depends on the answer to 'what viewpoint shall we take — one which will count the causes as "inside" or one which will count them as "outside"?' I do not know how retributionists would set about answering the last question, since it is not clear what criteria they have for answering it. But, again, it seems queer that the question of whether or not to punish a man should depend simply on what viewpoint we choose to adopt, when the reasons for such a choice are unclear.

These difficulties are not, of course, conclusive evidence against a belief in retribution: though they might well make the believer hesitate, if not change his mind. However, let us proceed on the assumption that we reject the need for 'punishment', 'judging', 'condemning', and 'finding guilty' as necessary moral features. If we do so, it seems that we must re-think our beliefs both in connection with sin and in connection with God's 'judgement'. We may now begin to think about placing the word 'judgement' inside inverted commas, so to speak.

We may easily (I think myself, rightly) come to the conclusion that our second sense of 'sin', whereby it seemed to be inextricably interwoven with the concept of freedom or free-will, should be assimilated more with the first sense, where it approximated rather to spiritual ill-health or disease. This leaves the question of whether or not a man is responsible for particular sins as an open question. We do not thereby shake the foundations of morality, or any other Christian beliefs. For those who are spiritually sick or diseased must 'pay the penalty': though we shall now understand this phrase as a metaphor from the law-courts. It would be preferable to say, indeed, that they do in fact 'pay the penalty': this is the sort of universe we live in, and surely the only possible sort. A universe where actions did not have consequences (and therefore evil actions evil consequences) is hardly conceivable.

We picture God, therefore, not as 'judging' and 'condemning' in a straightforward sense, but rather as approving a system whereby evil consequences follow from evil actions. This approval is now seen to be entirely natural and indeed inevitable. We do not now have to think of God condemning people whom He could absolve, were it not for the inexorable law of retribution: we think rather of Him sorrowing over those people who (whether as a result of their own free actions or not) are spiritually sick, and therefore suffer. This picture enables us to resolve typical conflicts, where we feel that God's judgement on sinners is not consistent with His everlasting mercy. We can believe, for instance, that some people may be permanently (though not, perhaps, irretrievably) sick, and may permanently suffer as a result of their sickness: there is nothing logically inconceivable in the notion that they may never recover. Nor, if we accept the inevitability of certain actions having certain consequences, must this seem morally repulsive. And this would enable us to believe in 'eternal punishment' or 'eternal damnation' in a very real sense, if we wish to do so. Only now we do not have to say that God deliberately 'condemns' people to damnation, with the implication that He could have let them off.

This sort of picture of 'sin' and 'judgement' seems to me far more consistent with what we believe about God's love and mercy. It does, however, clash with a picture which some of us still cherish. We tend to imagine that achieving salvation is largely a matter of avoiding sin and practising virtue: and in this we are in a sense correct. But we tend also to interpret 'sin' as the collecting of black marks, and 'virtue' as the scoring of points: both these activities being dependent solely upon ourselves or our own wills. According to this picture, life is a sort of gentlemanly cricket match, and God a sort of Divine Umpire. But this is hardly a realistic view. We do suffer, spiritually as well as otherwise, from the evil around us: though we also have the power to resist it. It is not the scoring of points that matters, but what we are. And this is not entirely a matter of free choice: though our free choices may be ultimately the most potent weapon in our armoury. Spiritual disease, like ordinary disease, is catching. I think that this point, if fully developed, would cause many of us to re-think our position in the world: particularly, perhaps, to realise our inter-dependence, and our membership of one body. We might come to take the command 'Judge not' rather more seriously; and we might spend less time in trying to assess guilt and inflict punishment, and more time in repelling that spiritual ill-health and disease which is in all of us, and for which 'sin' is the appropriate Christian referent.

FURTHER READING

I HAVE included in this list those works which are amongst the most helpful to those wishing to understand contemporary British philosophy in general, and its bearing upon religious belief in particular. Much — some would say, most — of the best writing in modern philosophy is to be found in various journals, which I have also mentioned.

BOOKS

Language, Truth and Logic	A. J. Ayer (Gollancz)
The Problem of Knowledge	A. J. Ayer (Macmillan)
Language and the Pursuit of Truth	John Wilson (C.U.P.)
New Essays in Philosophical Theology	
	(ed.) Flew and MacIntyre (S.C.M.)
Philosophy and Psychoanalysis	J. Wisdom (Basil Blackwell)
The Language of Morals	R. M. Hare (O.U.P.)
Ethics	P. Nowell Smith (Pelican)
Faith and Logic	(ed.) B. Mitchell (Allen & Unwin)

JOURNALS

Mind	(Thomas Nelson)
The Hibbert Journal	(Allen & Unwin)
The Philosophical Quarterly	(University of St. Andrews)

PRINTED IN GREAT BRITAIN BY ROBERT MACLEHOSE AND CO. LTD
THE UNIVERSITY PRESS, GLASGOW